Country Roads of

VIRGINIA

Country Roads of

VIRGINIA

Drives, Day Trips, and Weekend Excursions

Second Edition

Lynn Seldon

COUNTRY ROADS PRESS

NTC/Contemporary Publishing Group

Library of Congress Cataloging-in-Publication Data

Seldon, Lynn.
    Country roads of Virginia : drives, day trips, and weekend excursions /
by Lynn Seldon.—2nd ed.
        p.   cm.—(Country roads)
    Includes index.
    ISBN 1-56626-093-0
    1. Virginia—Tours.   2. Automobile travel—Virginia—Guidebooks.
3. Rural roads—Virginia—Guidebooks.   I. Title.   II. Series: Country
Roads (Series).
F224.3.S45   1999
917.5504'43—dc21   98-53358
                                           CIP

Cover and interior design by Nick Panos
Cover illustration copyright © Todd L. W. Doney
Interior site illustrations and map copyright © Leslie Faust
Interior spot illustrations copyright © Barbara Kelley
Picture research by Elizabeth Broadrup Lieberman

Published by Country Roads Press
A division of NTC/Contemporary Publishing Group, Inc.
4255 West Touhy Avenue, Lincolnwood (Chicago), Illinois 60646-1975 U.S.A.
Copyright © 1999, 1994 by Lynn Seldon
All rights reserved. No part of this book may be reproduced, stored in a retrieval
system, or transmitted in any form or by any means, electronic, mechanical,
photocopying, recording, or otherwise, without the prior permission of
NTC/Contemporary Publishing Group, Inc.
Printed in the United States of America
International Standard Book Number: 1-56626-093-0
99 00 01 02 03 ML 18 17 16 15 14 13 12 11 10 9 8 7 6 5 4 3 2 1

To Cele and my family and friends of the Old Dominion

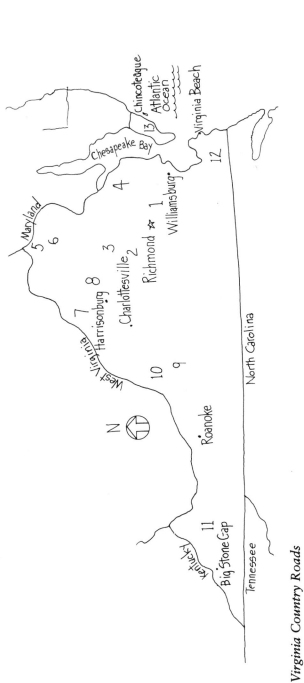

Virginia Country Roads
(Figures correspond with chapter numbers.)

Contents

Introduction

The popular tourism slogan "Virginia Is for Lovers" has so many meanings to me. It certainly has meant love in the traditional sense: I fell deeply in love and got married in the Old Dominion. But the slogan also means a love of everything the state has to offer. There's a lot to love: the history, the southern charm of the people and places, the mountains, the water, the big cities, the small towns, and the many country roads.

I was born and raised in Virginia and have lived in the state for all but six years of my life, when I was in the U.S. Army. My army time gave me a wanderlust that led to a career of travel. I'm a travel writer and photographer by trade and roam the world in search of a good story. But there's nothing better than roaming my own state on a country road.

Preparing this book renewed my immense love for everything this state has to offer. My companion for every mile and word was my soul mate and wife, Cele. When I refer to "we" in the text, you can assume it is the two of us. We've driven more than 4,000 miles in search of perfect country roads.

I've chosen a variety of routes that reflect the variety of experiences the state has to offer. In this book, you'll find a country road that will allow you to pursue almost any special love you have.

The interstate system helps you to get to Virginia's country roads quickly. That means you'll have more time to follow my recommendations and make many of your own discoveries as well. Allow yourself time to linger by planning to stay a night or more.

My research and travels for this book put me in contact with some great resources that can help other country road lovers. I highly recommend contacting tourism organizations for information and tips to make your own drives more enjoyable.

The Virginia Division of Tourism (1021 East Cary Street, Richmond, VA 23219, 804-786-2051 or 800-548-9797) is a wonderful resource for travel in the Old Dominion. Martha Steger and her staff were very helpful to me and will be happy to help you, too.

The Virginia Department of Agriculture and Consumer Services (P.O. Box 1163, Richmond, VA 23209, 804-786-0481) helps promote the state's agricultural products and wines. Contact it about the Virginia's Finest program for agricultural product promotion and for information about Virginia's wines and wineries.

I highly recommend staying in bed-and-breakfasts, small inns, and other local accommodations options throughout the state. Many excellent books about bed-and-breakfasts are available. Call 800-BNB-1293 for a free publication about Virginia's bed-and-breakfasts and country inns.

Many of the roads included here are part of the Virginia Byway system. You'll see many blue "Virginia Byway" signs, highlighted by a red cardinal, the state bird. The byways program recognizes certain roads for their historic or scenic interest, and Virginia has a lot of history and scenery to see.

Watch for the many historical markers throughout the state. *A Guidebook to Virginia's Historical Markers* (University Press of Virginia, Box 3608, University Station, Charlottesville, VA 22903, 804-924-6064) will help you choose which markers you'd like to visit before you even get in the car.

State parks (as well as several national parks) are prevalent along many of Virginia's country roads. Virginia has done an excellent job of promoting and preserving parks throughout the state. For more information about the state parks, contact the Department of Conservation and Recreation at 203 Governor Street, Suite 302, Richmond, VA 23219, 804-786-1712.

To simplify road designations, I've used the following abbreviations: I = Interstate; U.S. = U.S. Route or Highway; State = State Route or Highway; County = County Route or Road.

This book could not have been written without the help of many people. Everywhere we went, we told people about the project, and they did their best to help us make this book better for future visitors.

Many of my friends in Richmond contributed some great ideas that made their way into the book. My parents and family contributed a love of their state and support of the travel-writing dream that I have somehow made a reality.

My wife, Cele, has been there for me, on the road and at the computer, for the entire project. In many ways, this book is a joint project and a gift of thanks to the state for having so many wonderful country roads to explore. We hope you'll agree with Thomas Jefferson, who said, "On the whole, I find nothing anywhere else . . . which Virginia need envy."

Country Roads of

VIRGINIA

1

Plantation Road

Getting there: From Richmond (west to east), take Main Street east out of downtown and follow the signs for Williamsburg and State 5. Alternatively, take I-95 south to I-295 east, then follow State 5 east just outside the city. From Williamsburg (west to east), take State 5 out of Colonial Williamsburg and follow the signs for Richmond via State 5 west.

Highlights: Pick just one or two plantations of interest and explore them thoroughly. Take the time to stay in one of the bed-and-breakfasts along the route. Alternatively, include a tour of Richmond or the "Historic Triangle" of Colonial Williamsburg, Yorktown, and Jamestown. This drive is easily completed in one or two days.

In less than 60 miles, the road between Richmond and Williamsburg winds through more than 300 years of Virginia (and U.S.) history. The drive is like a trip to visit some wealthy friends at their large country estate.

Richmond and Williamsburg are connected by much more than a beautiful country road. Williamsburg was the original state capital, before the Old Dominion's headquarters was moved to Richmond. Now nearby I-64 makes the trip a blur at 65 MPH. But State 5 allows you to linger in the present and take glimpses into the past.

As you leave Richmond along the James River, the modern skyline looms in your rearview mirror, and the past is just a few miles down the road. One mile out of town, the *Annabel Lee,* a restored paddle wheeler, sits on the James waiting to take groups along the scenic river. You can also sign up nearby for a white-water rafting trip through downtown Richmond.

Civil War buffs flock to Fort Harrison, one of many large battlefields that are part of the Richmond National Battlefield Park. The park has a small museum and visitors center, where you can pick up background on Fort Harrison's role in the Civil War and a useful map.

Fort Harrison was bloodily captured by Union forces under Gen. Ulysses S. Grant in 1864. The battle was the beginning of the downfall of Richmond, the capital of the Confederacy, six months later. It's a pretty and peaceful walking tour and drive through the park before heading back to State 5.

Most drivers are drawn to the large number of Virginia historic markers along this route. Cars are constantly pulling over for roadside history lessons, culled from the distinctive signs all along Virginia's historic roads.

For instance, upon entering Charles City County, we learned that the area was one of eight shires formed in 1634 and that two U.S. presidents (John Tyler and William Henry Harrison) were born here. A bit farther down the road, a historic marker notes that Thomas Jefferson married Martha Wayles Skelton in her home nearby (called The Forest) and that they then rode in the snow to Monticello.

"Signseers" (as opposed to sightseers) will also notice the attractive "Virginia Byway" signs (with a cardinal, the state bird) denoting the historic and scenic importance of this road. You'll see these signs often on the country roads described in this book.

Only 18 miles and hundreds of years out of Richmond is the first of many plantations. A tree-lined road leads to Shirley Plantation. Shirley was founded in 1613, just six years after the settlers arrived in Jamestown to establish the first permanent English colony in the New World. The brick structure is one of the nation's prime examples of Queen Anne architecture.

It has been the home of the Carter family since 1723. The 800-acre working plantation is now owned and operated by the ninth and tenth generations of the original family. It was the home of Anne Hill Carter, mother of Robert E. Lee.

Many prominent Virginians, including George Washington and Thomas Jefferson, enjoyed the hospitality of Shirley Plantation. Look for the plethora of pineapples, a colonial symbol of hospitality, in the hand-carved woodwork of the house and the three-and-a-half-foot pineapple finial on the peak of the roof. The history- and anecdote-packed tour is excellent, and a tour of the grounds along the James River is invigorating.

Just down the road on the left is one of the best "nonplantation" stops along State 5. Edgewood Bed and Breakfast is a perfect place to find some southern hospitality, antique shopping, and, of course, a bed for the night and a full breakfast in the morning.

Julian and Dot Boulware play host in this historic house, which has served as a church, post office, telephone exchange, restaurant, nursing home, and lookout for Confederate generals. I think it is now enjoying its best use.

Eight well-appointed rooms are offered, all packed with antiques and history. Behind the main house, Prissy's Quarters is a separate retreat for romantic couples. Edgewood has a pool, hot tub, and gazebo. Dot provides a wealth of local lore and can arrange special outings for guests. Country road lovers should take time to stop in for a few minutes . . . or the night.

A few miles farther on the right are two plantations for the price of one turn down a country road. Berkeley Plantation is

Berkeley Plantation

one of the most popular stops on State 5, and Westover Plantation's nearby grounds feature a peaceful stroll along the James River.

The half-mile dirt road to Berkeley was designed for carriages and built in 1725. A sign asks drivers to drive "leisurely."

Good Housekeeping suggested, "If you only have time for one plantation, Berkeley should be at the top of your list," and Virginia senator Charles Robb said, "If you haven't been to Berkeley, you haven't lived." It gets my "seal of approval," too. This historic mansion was built in 1726 (the initials of Benjamin Harrison IV and his wife, Anne, are on a date stone over a side door) and has since played host to George Washington, the succeeding nine U.S. presidents, and thousands of plantation-loving tourists.

The colonial-clad tour guides will point out many interesting facts. We learned that "Taps" was composed at Berkeley in 1862 while Union forces were camped at the plantation. We also learned that William Henry Harrison, Gov. Benjamin Harrison's third son, was born at Berkeley. The younger Harrison went on to become a famous Indian fighter, the ninth president of the United States, and the grandfather of the 23rd president of the United States, Benjamin Harrison.

In the gift shop, I found a great book about Berkeley, *The Grand Plantation* by Clifford Dowdey. The animated woman at the counter told me about the Virginia First Thanksgiving Festival, an annual celebration on the first Sunday in November. In 1619, Capt. John Woodlief came safely ashore here (two years before the colonists arrived in Massachusetts), and Virginians have since celebrated the event yearly, as directed in the group's original instructions:

> Wee ordained that the day of our ships arrivall at the place assigned for plantacon in the land of Virginia shall be yearly and perpetually keept holy as a day of thanksgiving to Almight God.

This popular event includes historical reenactments, crafts, Native American dancers and exhibits, music, and some great Virginia food. It's a perfect time to be on State 5. If you can't make it for the festival, try a meal in Berkeley's Coach House Tavern, where the first 10 U.S. presidents dined.

By taking the other fork on the road to Berkeley, you can go to Westover Plantation. Only the grounds of this home, built about 1730 by William Byrd II, are open for touring, but it's definitely worth the drive and the walk.

Westover is situated directly on the James River. The best view of the buildings and grounds is found by walking across the lawn instead of following the path. Check out the small structure by the icehouse, which contains passageways leading to the river in case of attack by Indians.

On the other side of the house, look for the iron fence with supporting columns topped by unusual stone finials cut to resemble an acorn for perseverance (from little acorns great oaks grow), a pineapple for hospitality, a Greek Key to the World for knowledge, a cornucopia (horn of plenty), a beehive for industry, and an urn of flowers for beauty.

Back on State 5, immediately look for the turn to Westover Church. The original church was built nearby in 1613. The current site and building date to 1730. If you're enjoying State 5 on a Sunday, you may attend church services at 11:00 A.M.

Even if you've seen enough plantations, take the road up to Evelynton. It's worth the drive to visit the wonderful gift shop and greenhouse. Originally part of William Byrd's Westover Plantation (he named it for his daughter Evelyn), it has been in the Ruffin family since 1847.

If you tour the grounds and house, you'll learn some fascinating facts about the history of the plantation and the Ruffin family. The family's patriarch, Edmund Ruffin, is said to have fired the first shot of the Civil War at Fort Sumter. He earned the title "Father of American Agronomy" by saving 19th-century Virginia from a depressed agricultural economy.

Time your drive so that you end up at Indian Fields Tavern for a meal. Just three miles east of Evelynton, this restored farmhouse is gaining national recognition for its creative southern hospitality and fare. Sample the peanut soup, some Smithfield ham, the homemade Sally Lunn bread, and one of the homemade desserts. The restaurant is open for lunch and dinner and is run by Archer Ruffin of the famed Ruffin family.

Just 10 minutes farther along, stop for the night at North Bend Plantation B&B. George and Ridgely Copland restored this lovely Greek Revival house in 1984. Highlights of any visit include an incredible collection of old and rare books, stunning antiques, and a full country breakfast with mouth-watering homemade waffles.

The final plantation along this stretch of State 5 is Sherwood Forest Plantation, and it's an interesting one. Sherwood Forest was the home of President John Tyler and is considered the longest frame house in America (300 feet). It has been a working plantation for more than 240 years and is still occupied by members of the Tyler family. Check out the Pet Grave Yard and the names of past Tyler family pets.

A few miles after Sherwood Forest, civilization and the 20th century loom ahead. Cars enter James City County by a drawbridge over the wide Chickahominy River, and more signs of modern life (as in billboards and commercialism) lure drivers off the country road. Real-estate developments and the Williamsburg Pottery, a legendary outlet shopping mecca, are just a few reminders that plantation life has ended.

State 5 heads into Williamsburg. Stop by the College of William and Mary or head to any point of the Historic Triangle. The drive officially ends at Merchant's Square in Colonial Williamsburg, where you'll find some great shopping and incredible meals at The Trellis.

For More Information

Annabel Lee (Richmond): 804-644-5700 or 800-752-7093

Richmond National Battlefield Park: 804-226-1981

Shirley Plantation (Charles City): 800-232-1613

Edgewood Bed and Breakfast (Charles City): 804-829-2962

Berkeley Plantation (Charles City): 804-829-6018

Westover Plantation (Charles City): 804-829-2882

Evelynton (Charles City): 800-473-5075

Indian Fields Tavern (Charles City): 804-829-5004

North Bend Plantation B&B (Charles City): 804-829-5176

Sherwood Forest Plantation (Charles City): 804-829-5377

Williamsburg Pottery (Lightfoot): 757-564-3326

The Trellis (Williamsburg): 757-229-8610

2

Into Jefferson Country

Getting there: From Richmond (east to west), take Patterson Avenue (State 6) west out of downtown. Alternatively, take I-95 north or I-64 west to the Parham Road West exit, continue to Patterson Avenue (State 6), and turn right (west). From Charlottesville, follow State 20 south out of town.

Highlights: A meal at the North Pole; rolling Virginia farmland and horse country; James River; historic town of Scottsville; visiting a Virginia vineyard; Michie Tavern; Thomas Jefferson's Monticello. This drive is easily completed in one or two days.

Thomas Jefferson loved the rolling countryside of central Virginia and roamed the region in search of beautiful scenery, architectural possibilities, and vineyard sites. Today's roamers can do the same on the roads from Richmond to Charlottesville and into Jefferson country.

The switch from city to country life is swift on the road out of Richmond. Patterson Avenue quickly changes from urban to suburban to not-at-all-urban. The road narrows to two lanes at the Hermitage Country Club, a sure sign that better driving is ahead.

Many Richmonders head out this way in the evening for a meal at the North Pole in Crozier. This legendary eatery features huge, tasty, panfried steaks in a casual atmosphere. It's an ideal destination if you're spending the night in or around Richmond before or after a drive into Jefferson country. Another option just a bit farther west is Tanglewood Ordinary, offering family-style country cooking for one all-you-can-eat price.

Goochland is the ideal place to meet a few locals, and there's no better place than the Goochland Restaurant. Many farmers and other folks from around the area can be found here discussing world and local events over a cup of coffee or a meal. This is also a great place for heading down to the James River for some peace and quiet.

The drive west of Goochland is filled with rolling farmland and attractive scenery. Look for Big Lickinghole Creek and Little Lickinghole Creek. There's a taxidermist on the left if you want a wild souvenir from your drive.

The next stop is Columbia, a relatively small, deserted town where you can explore the old storefronts and train station. At one time, no doubt, Columbia was a hopping town.

In Fork Union, State 6 makes a sharp turn right. Drivers in the know stay straight for another hundred yards or so to check out Fork Union Military Academy on the left side of U.S. 15. Founded in 1898, this stark and stately military school is a great place to park for a talk with a few of the cadets.

Head back to State 6 and the road to Scottsville. Historic Scottsville was once called Scott's Landing, and it's easy to see why, with the James River lapping at the town limits at the "Famous Horseshoe Bend."

Your first stop should be the Scottsville Museum, which houses an interesting collection of town memorabilia and antiques. The museum was originally a Disciples Church, built in 1846. The Barclay House next door was the home of Dr. James Turner Barclay, who founded the church, was its first preacher, and went on to become a missionary to Jerusalem and author of *The City of the Great King.*

Scottsville was originally a center for the corn-growing Monacan Indians. In the 18th century, it became the county seat and served as an important river gateway to the Appalachians. The 19th century brought boom days along the river and Kanawha Canal before the Civil War brought destruction.

Today Scottsville still features 32 Federal-style buildings, one of the largest concentrations in the state. The town is perfect for parking, walking, and talking to friendly locals. Make sure to find the Federal-style stores along Valley Street, the Tobacco Warehouse, Old Hall, Bruce House, Old Tavern, Tompkins House, Mount Walla, Cliffside, and the Presbyterian Church.

If all this walking makes you hungry, stop by the Pig & Steak Too on Valley Street, dubbed the "Original Dew Drop Inn." If you're really tuckered out or time it just right, stay the night at the High Meadows Inn. This classic hillside European-style auberge features 23 acres of tranquility, spacious 19th-century bedrooms, private baths, and fireplaces. Hosts Peter Sushka and Jae Abbitt also offer a full country breakfast, weekday evening supper baskets, twilight Virginia wine-tasting parties, and romantic weekend candlelight dining.

You leave Scottsville toward Charlottesville along the Constitution Route. This famous part of State 20, stretching for 90 miles, was officially named in 1975 to recognize its historic significance to the state and the nation. Four U.S. presidents—Jefferson, Madison, Monroe, and Taylor—either were born or built their private estates along this route. So did 11 Virginia governors, from colonial times to the present.

A great way to toast all this history is at one of the many Virginia wineries in the area. On State 20, turn left onto County 720 (follow the grape signs) toward Horton Cellars. One of Virginia's largest wineries, Horton features more than

50 acres of vineyards. The underground winery is built into the side of a hill and is capable of producing 50,000 gallons of wine per year. Horton's tours and tastings are among the best in Virginia.

Back on State 20, you'll find one of the most interesting dining experiences in Virginia. Just outside Charlottesville, follow the signs at State 53 for Historic Michie Tavern and Monticello.

Michie Tavern was originally built in 1784 by William Michie to accommodate the many travelers needing food and shelter along a well-traveled stagecoach route. It was owned and operated by his descendants for more than 150 years.

Today the Michie Tavern complex still offers travelers great food and exploration opportunities. The focus of any visit is "The Ordinary." This colonial buffet offers traditional dishes such as fried chicken, black-eyed peas, stewed tomatoes, coleslaw, potato salad, green bean salad, Tavern beets, homemade biscuits, corn bread, the tavern's special apple cobbler, and Virginia wines and ales to slake your thirst. The Michie Tavern serves meals seven days a week from 11:30 A.M. to 3:00 P.M.

The Tavern Museum offers tours of the 18th-century inn, including the Ballroom, "Private Quarters," Keeping Hall, Ladies and Gentlemen's Parlor, and outbuildings. The Wine Cellar houses the Virginia Wine Museum.

Down the hill, the old Meadow Run Grist Mill is now the General Store, offering an array of shopping possibilities. An old mercantile atmosphere prevails, with a cigar-store Indian, checkerboard ready for play, post office, barbershop, and rare collection of Americana.

Just down the road is Thomas Jefferson's mountaintop home, Monticello (Italian for "little mountain"). Jefferson was the third president of the United States, author of the Declaration

Monticello

of Independence, governor of Virginia, and founder of Charlottesville's University of Virginia. He designed and built Monticello between 1768 and 1809.

The tour and services at Monticello are among the best in the state. Visitors' eyes are drawn first to the dramatic dome (it appears on the back of the U.S. nickel). The Thomas Jefferson Memorial Foundation has meticulously restored the house, grounds, gardens, and other buildings to their original state.

Most of the furnishings in the house were owned by Jefferson or his family. Look for gadgets throughout, including the seven-day clock in the entrance hall and the single-acting double doors in the parlor. The guided tour of the first floor includes many highlights, such as the bed where Jefferson died on July 4, 1826, 50 years after the signing of the Declaration of Independence.

Monticello's gardens and outbuildings are also fun to explore. The gardens are laid out just as Jefferson had them.

The hillside outbuildings include a smokehouse, an icehouse, servants' quarters, stables, and Jefferson's "bachelor's quarters." His grave is in the family graveyard just below the house.

Ash Lawn, the relatively simple plantation home of James Monroe, is two miles past Monticello. This plantation was named for the prevalent great ash trees on the property. The house was designed and built by Monroe's friend Jefferson in 1799.

Monroe was the fifth president of the United States; secretary of state and war; a U.S. senator; and minister to England, Spain, and France (he negotiated the Louisiana Purchase). He also authored the Monroe Doctrine.

Ash Lawn's furnishings are modest, showing that Monroe did not become wealthy as a farmer's son and public servant. The beautiful boxwood garden is more than a century old and affords a great view of Monticello.

Back on State 20, make sure to stop by the Thomas Jefferson Visitors Center just before the I-64 interchange. This helpful stop includes the "Thomas Jefferson at Monticello" historic exhibit, maps and brochures, and people to answer all sorts of questions.

The road leads on to Charlottesville, a beautiful college town. It is the home of the University of Virginia and has become a state cultural center. Visit the university's Rotunda and lawns and the Bayly Museum. Jefferson would have been proud.

For More Information

North Pole (Crozier): 804-784-4222

Tanglewood Ordinary (Maidens): 804-556-3284

High Meadows Inn (Scottsville): 804-286-2218

Horton Cellars (Charlottesville): 540-832-7440

Michie Tavern (Charlottesville): 804-977-1234

Monticello (Charlottesville): 804-984-9800

Ash Lawn (Charlottesville): 804-293-9539

3

The Constitution Route

Getting there: From Richmond, take I-64 west approximately 70 miles to Charlottesville, then take the State 20 exit for the Constitution Route (west to east). From Washington, D.C., take I-95 south about 60 miles to Fredericksburg, then take the State 3 exit at Fredericksburg. The drive (backward) begins here.

Highlights: Charlottesville; horse country; the Burnley and Barboursville vineyards and wineries; James Madison's Montpelier; Orange; and Civil War battlefields and history between Orange and Fredericksburg. This drive is easily completed in one or two days.

The Constitution Route technically runs from Appomattox to Fredericksburg (a portion of it is covered in Chapter 2). State 20 was officially named the "Constitution Route" in 1975.

Four U.S. presidents—Jefferson, Madison, Monroe, and Taylor—were either born or built their private estates along or near the drive. Jefferson once said, "Too many scenes of happiness mingle themselves with all my recollections of my native woods and fields." From colonial times to the present, 11 Virginia governors also have been born or lived along the route.

This portion of the Constitution Route begins in the college town of Charlottesville. State 20 winds out of Charlottesville and the academic environment into an area of horse farms and large country estates. The rolling hills of Albemarle County play host to old and new money (and some big homes).

The 20-minute drive to Barboursville is highlighted by two vineyards and wineries. The first is Burnley Vineyards, found two miles before Barboursville after a left turn onto County 641. Burnley makes some of the state's best wines.

Burnley's tasting room and banquet area overlook the vineyards and provide an ideal setting for an educational and enjoyable tasting. We particularly liked the Rivanna White and Rivanna Sunset (a blush wine made from Chambourcin grapes) and the friendly winery dogs. The owners, the Reeder family, also rent a wonderful chalet-style house in the vineyards that sleeps four.

Just up the road, take a right onto County 678, follow it for one-half mile, and then turn right onto County 777 (Vineyard Road). There you'll find Barboursville Vineyards, which has played a big role in the growing popularity of Virginia wines. The Zonin family established Barboursville in 1976, and the winery has hosted thousands of visitors since.

Barboursville's shop offers excellent tastings, tours, and sales. We particularly liked the award-winning chardonnays and the Rieslings.

We almost didn't stop by the Barboursville "mansion," but that would have been a big mistake. The mansion was one of the largest and finest residences in the region before it was destroyed by fire on Christmas Day, 1884. It was constructed between 1814 and 1822 and was the only building in Orange County known to have been designed by Thomas Jefferson. It was built for his friend James Barbour, a Virginia governor,

U.S. senator, secretary of war, and ambassador to England. The picturesque and peaceful ruins are a joy to explore.

State 20 intersects U.S. 33 at Barboursville, then continues northeast to Orange and a lot more history. This is James Madison country, and the Madison family graveyard serves as a perfect prelude to his house. It's located about six miles before Orange and is well marked. An old wooden bridge (it doesn't look as if it will support a car, but it will) leads to the peaceful cemetery where Madison and his wife, Dolley, are buried.

Montpelier, the home of James Madison, our fourth president, is located just four miles southwest of Orange on State 20. Park at Montpelier Station, which has a great little "general store" and shuttle buses to the estate.

Madison was a chief proponent of the Bill of Rights and the "Father of the Constitution." He was the third generation of his family to live at Montpelier.

The property was opened for public tours in 1987, as part of the bicentennial celebration of the U.S. Constitution. The tour of Montpelier is an exploration of preservation in progress, as the house is still unfurnished and unrestored.

Admission includes a bus tour of the 2,700-acre estate, a guided tour of the mansion and archaeological and architectural research, and a self-guided tree and garden walk. The estate has 40 species of trees from around the world and a beautiful formal garden that is being restored by the Garden Club of Virginia.

Orange is a typically charming Virginia town and deserves several hours (or a night or weekend) of exploration. Orange County once stretched as far west as the Mississippi River and as far north as the Great Lakes.

In Orange, the James Madison Museum features four permanent exhibits on Madison's life, his family, Virginia, and the United States. Madison artifacts include furnishings from Montpelier, correspondence, fashions associated with Dolley Madison, and books from Madison's library.

Special exhibits are presented on a regular basis at the excellent museum, which also includes the unusual Hall of Agricultural Progress. Many farm implements and machines are on display there. Madison was an innovative farmer. Jefferson once referred to him as "the best farmer in the world."

Located near the James Madison Museum is the Orange County Visitors Center, which offers information on the area's sights, accommodations, and amenities. Just next door is St. Thomas Episcopal Church, the only surviving example of Jefferson's church architecture.

The Orange County Historical Society is just across the street. The research library, archives, and friendly staff can answer almost any question about Orange County history.

Although a fire destroyed much of the town in 1908, many other historic homes and buildings remain. Look for the Court House, the Sparks Building, and the Taliaferro House on Main Street; Peliso on Peliso Avenue; and Rebel Hall on May Fray Avenue, a gathering place for Confederate officers.

This quaint town offers much more to explore, and the best bet is to choose a bed-and-breakfast for the night (or longer). Two great choices are located right in town. The Holladay House at 155 West Main Street is a restored Federal-style home that has been in the Holladay family since 1899. Pete and Phebe Holladay are charming hosts and will enhance any Orange County visit. Pete is very active in the Bed and Breakfast Association of Virginia, so he can recommend other bed-and-breakfasts throughout the Old Dominion.

The Victorian-style Hidden Inn at 249 Caroline Street features 10 guest rooms, a home-cooked country breakfast, afternoon tea, dinner by candlelight, and the friendliness of Ray and Barbara Lonick. Just a mile southwest of town is The Shadows, a small stone bed-and-breakfast with four rooms, a cabin, and a cottage. Pat and Barbara Loffredo pamper their guests beyond the call of duty. Ask to see the Victorian Room, the Rocking Horse Cabin, and the Cottage.

Leaving Orange is difficult, but State 20 still has much in store. Civil War history abounds along the rest of this route and on into Fredericksburg on State 3. Many historic markers describe the Civil War action in the area, including the Mine Run Campaign, where Robert E. Lee's troops engaged the right wing of Ulysses S. Grant's army in late November 1863, successfully blocking their march south.

About 25 miles from Orange, you can tour the Wilderness Civil War Battlefield by car. The vicious battle here on May 5–6, 1864, resulted in more than 26,000 casualties and marked General Grant's first step toward Appomattox. The tour starts at the Wilderness Exhibit Shelter one mile west of State 3.

The Constitution Route technically ends at State 3, but more history drew us on toward Fredericksburg. Just after we turned right onto State 3, the well-tended National Park Service's Chancellorsville Battlefield Visitor Center beckoned.

Chancellorsville is a mecca for Civil War buffs. This battle is considered by many to be Lee's greatest victory, as his outnumbered troops fought valiantly there for three days. Lee's forces suffered more than 30,000 casualties, including the death of Gen. Thomas "Stonewall" Jackson. The excellent visitors center provides a great introduction to the battle and other information, including Park Service tapes for touring the park by car.

About six miles along toward Fredericksburg is the Salem Church, which served as the focal point of the Battle of Chancellorsville. The restored church still sports battle scars on its walls. The drive ends in the historic haven of Fredericksburg. Although it's a commonly used phrase throughout the state, George Washington really did sleep here. He lived on a farm right outside the city, where the legendary cherry tree incident occurred. His sister lived in Fredericksburg, and he visited often. Follow the signs to the Fredericksburg Visitor Center at 706 Caroline Street for ideas. (See Chapter 4.)

For More Information

Burnley Vineyards (Barboursville): 540-832-2828

Barboursville Vineyards: 540-832-3824

Montpelier, Orange County: 540-672-2728

James Madison Museum (Orange): 540-672-1776

Orange County Historical Society (Orange): 540-672-5366

Holladay House (Orange): 540-672-4893 or 800-358-4422

Hidden Inn (Orange): 540-672-3625

The Shadows (Orange): 540-672-5057

Wilderness Civil War Battlefield, Orange County: 540-373-4461

Chancellorsville Battlefield Visitor Center: 540-786-2880

Fredericksburg Visitor Center: 540-373-1776 or 800-678-4748

4

The Northern Neck

Getting there: From Washington, D.C., take I-95 south to Fredericksburg and State 3 and the start of the drive. From Richmond, take I-95 north to Fredericksburg and State 3 and the start of the drive.

Highlights: Fredericksburg; Westmoreland Berry Farm; Ingleside Plantation Vineyards; Colonial Beach; George Washington Birthplace National Monument; Stratford Hall Plantation; Montross Inn & Restaurant; Lowery's Seafood Restaurant; Christ Church; Irvington. This drive can be completed in one long day.

It's amazing what getting off the interstate can do for the mind, body, and soul. Almost anywhere in the state, a country road beckons just off the highway. For instance, many I-95 drivers don't know about the more peaceful drive along the Northern Neck.

This road starts in the historic haven of Fredericksburg. State 3 leads right through this interesting city, which is definitely worth a stop if you have time. It's also a great place to spend the night before getting an early start to the Northern Neck the next morning.

Fredericksburg is great for walking and driving, with much to see in a small space. We headed straight for the Fredericksburg Visitor Center at 706 Caroline Street, where we picked up a map and specific touring recommendations.

In the city center, our first stop was the Hugh Mercer Apothecary Shop at 1020 Caroline Street. Opened in 1771, it is one of the oldest apothecary shops in the nation. Dr. Mercer practiced medicine and ran the pharmacy. The shop has been restored to its 18th-century appearance and features medicine bottles, pills, and prescriptions.

The Rising Sun Tavern at 1306 Caroline Street was the social and political center of early Fredericksburg. It was built by George Washington's youngest brother, Charles, in 1760 and played host to most of the key colonial patriots. The restored building now features the Tap Room (with whale-bone checkers) and the gentlemen's chambers, where four men might have had to sleep in one small bed.

The James Monroe Law Office and Museum at 908 Charles Street marks the site of the start of Monroe's successful private and public career. Monroe would eventually hold more high offices than any other president. The most interesting item on display is a Louis XVI desk, which was used for the signing of the Monroe Doctrine.

The Mary Washington House, purchased by George for his mother, contains many of Mrs. Washington's belongings. Don't miss the beautiful English garden in the back. (Look for her sundial and the boxwood she planted long ago.) Her peaceful grave site and monument is on Washington Avenue, at the end of Pitt Street.

Kenmore, at 1201 Washington Avenue, was the elegant 18th-century plantation home of George Washington's only sister, Betty. The highlight of the Information Center is a huge diorama of Fredericksburg as it was in 1765. The guided tour of this large house includes many Washington family artifacts and much insight into 18th-century plantation life.

If you wish to spend the night in Fredericksburg before or after exploring the Northern Neck, you'll find several lodging and dining options. In keeping with the historic theme, we liked the Fredericksburg Colonial Inn at 1707 Princess Anne Street. This 30-room Civil War–era inn is located in the historic district.

For a great period meal (as well as nice accommodations), head for the Kenmore Inn at 1200 Princess Anne Street. The Kenmore is a romantic and historic inn, restaurant, and pub. We also took time to shop at the Made in Virginia Shop at 807 Caroline Street. It's the perfect place to find a gift from the Old Dominion.

The country road drive starts in earnest just outside Fredericksburg on State 3. The road winds through farmland and past many historic markers. Just a mile or so along, look for the markers for Chatham and Washington's boyhood home.

Chatham, built about 1750, was where Robert E. Lee came to court his wife. During the Civil War, it was occupied by Generals Edwin Sumner and Joseph Hooker.

Washington's boyhood home, Ferry Farm, was the place where legend says he cut down the cherry tree. He lived there from 1739 to 1747. His father died there in 1743, but his mother stayed on the farm until 1771.

State 3 continues through King George, crosses over U.S. 301, and enters the Northern Neck in earnest. State 3 serves as the main road, but this drive requires a lot of turnoffs to many points of interest.

The first such turnoff is a tasty turn-on. The Westmoreland Berry Farm (right on County 634, which turns into County 637) can provide a fun feast. This huge riverside farm and orchard near Oak Grove features a fresh farm market, related products, pick-your-own crops, and many enjoyable special events.

You can enjoy the fruits of other people's labor or the fruits of your own in a fun and friendly atmosphere. In 1983,

Chuck and Anne Geyer began transforming the farm for the Vorhees family. Today they offer a truly special Northern Neck experience.

Take a right back out on County 637, then take a left onto County 638 to one of Virginia's best wineries. Ingleside Plantation Vineyards is a great place to visit. Ingleside has a nice tasting area and gift shops, group tours, and a wonderful courtyard for picnicking and wine tasting.

Carl Flemer planted the first grapes at Ingleside in 1960, and his homemade wine became a local favorite. He expanded the operation and attained commercial status in 1980. Jacques Recht, a Belgian, French-trained enologist, turned Ingleside into an award-winning winery.

Jacques and his wife, Liliane, had taken early retirement and were sailing around the world when they decided to explore the area they had read about in James Michener's *Chesapeake*. When they met Carl Flemer, a three-week consultation visit turned into a passion. Recht is now the resident wine master and a consultant to other wineries from Virginia to New York.

Back on State 3, you'll find many more fascinating turnoffs just down the road. For instance, Colonial Beach is a short drive north on State 205. This quaint Victorian town is one of the few remaining seaport towns on the Potomac River. At one time, it was a popular summer resort and a favorite retreat for Alexander Graham Bell. Today it is experiencing a rebirth, with a renovated beachfront, a variety of accommodations, and great seafood restaurants.

Back on State 3 again, you'll come to the George Washington Birthplace National Monument, which offers some interesting insights into "The Father of Our Country." This park, efficiently run by the National Park Service, features a working 18th-century farm and plantation, many museum exhibits, and the memorial house (not the original one) with costumed interpreters. It's well worth the admission price.

Just up State 347 is Westmoreland State Park, a real find in a state packed with excellent parks. This hilly site on the Potomac River is popular for swimming, hiking, biking, picnicking, and camping. You can also rent a cabin if you wish. Stay one night or an entire week.

Next in line is Robert E. Lee's birthplace, Stratford Hall Plantation, just off State 3 on State 214 north. Thomas Lee, Robert's great-uncle, built this beautiful colonial home and plantation on a bluff overlooking the Potomac River.

Thomas Lee's sons included Richard Henry Lee and Francis Lightfoot Lee, both of whom signed the Declaration of Independence. Their cousin, Revolutionary War hero Henry "Light-Horse Harry" Lee, lived at Stratford for more than 20 years.

Stratford's most famous resident was Henry Lee's son Robert, born in a big, sunlit upstairs bedroom. You can still see the crib where Robert slept. The rest of the house and grounds are packed with interesting relics and reminders of a long-gone era. A log cabin dining room offers a plantation lunch from April to November.

State 3 continues on through the middle of the Northern Neck to Montross. This town has two places worth checking out: the Montross Inn & Restaurant and the Westmoreland County Museum and Visitor Center.

The Montross Inn & Restaurant, run by Eileen and Michael Longman, draws loyal visitors from afar with a European-inn atmosphere. It's a perfect place for lunch, dinner, or the night. Just down the street, the small county museum features historical displays and friendly hosts anxious to help you enjoy your visit to the Northern Neck.

Warsaw is a quaint Northern Neck town that serves as the Richmond County seat. The county courthouse has been here since 1748, as has the clerk's office, which is still heated by the original open fireplace.

On a whim, we took a detour from State 3 and headed over the Rappahannock River to the town of Tappahannock. Tappahannock started as a port town in 1680 and has developed into a Northern Neck gateway for country road drivers.

Our target was Lowery's Seafood Restaurant, a Virginia tradition since 1938. This large, friendly place serves simple seafood in heaping portions. Lowery's has a loyal following from throughout the state.

If you have time, take U.S. 360 from Warsaw into the northern section of the region. Two wonderful historic sites, as well as the wonderful town of Reedville, are located in the area. Reedville offers the quintessential Northern Neck experience, as well as the Reedville Fisherman's Museum and popular cruises to Smith Island and Tangier Island, choice Chesapeake Bay destinations.

If you choose not to explore the northern section, State 3 meanders on through the countryside, passing through Lively, where you'll find Karen's Lively Bakery and Lively Drugs, and Lancaster. Look for the Mary Ball Washington Museum & Library in Lancaster, which highlights the life of George Washington's mother.

In Kilmarnock, follow State 200 to Christ Church. It's well worth the detour. Historic Christ Church is the only virtually unchanged colonial church in America, and it's a beauty.

It was built in a beautiful setting by Robert "King" Carter between 1730 and 1734 and has been continuously used for services since 1850. The church has been carefully restored and features entrancing brickwork, windows, and pews and a rare three-deck pulpit. The modern Reception Center provides the perfect introduction to the church.

In 1971, the church won one of the first two awards of

the National Trust for Historic Preservation. The citation stated, "The Foundation's ten-year program of historical, architectural, and archeological research has culminated in a restoration that is one of the most scholarly and outstanding in the country and one of the nation's great monuments of religion and architecture."

The Tides Inn at Irvington provides an abrupt but elegant leap into the 20th century. This classy waterfront resort offers great accommodations, golf, dining, and many other amenities. The Tides Lodge, a sister resort, is located nearby.

State 3 heads across the Rappahannock and back to civilization. But you won't soon forget the Northern Neck's country roads.

For More Information

Fredericksburg Visitor Center: 540-373-1776 or 800-678-4748

Fredericksburg Colonial Inn: 540-371-5666

Kenmore Inn (Fredericksburg): 540-371-7622

Made in Virginia Shop (Fredericksburg): 540-371-2030 or 800-635-3149

Westmoreland Berry Farm (Oak Grove): 804-224-9171

Ingleside Plantation Vineyards (Oak Grove): 804-224-8687

Colonial Beach Chamber of Commerce: 804-224-4185

George Washington Birthplace National Monument (Montross): 804-224-1732

Westmoreland State Park (Montross): 804-493-8821

Stratford Hall Plantation (Montross): 804-493-8038 or 804-493-8371

Montross Inn & Restaurant: 804-493-0573

Westmoreland County Museum and Visitor Center (Montross):
804-493-8440

Lowery's Seafood Restaurant (Tappahannock): 804-443-2800

Reedville Fisherman's Museum: 804-453-6529

Mary Ball Washington Museum & Library (Lancaster):
804-462-7280

Historic Christ Church (Irvington): 804-438-6855

The Tides Inn and the Tides Lodge (Irvington): 800-TIDES INN
or 800-843-3746

5

A D.C. Day Drive

Getting there: From Washington, take State 7 west about one hour to begin the drive.

Highlights: Waterford; Taylorstown General Store; Lovettsville; Hillsboro. This drive can easily be completed in one day, but the area deserves a weekend or more.

Some drives are meant to be savored for their pure scenic beauty rather than the stops along the way. This is one of those drives. It's short, and there are only a few stops, but it sure is sweet.

The drive begins just outside Purcellville on County 622 north toward the town of Waterford. This area of Loudoun County is known as Virginia's Hunt Country ("where tradition is more than a memory," according to a tourism brochure), and this Virginia Byway offers curvy driving and rolling countryside (great for foxes and the traditional "hunt"). You'll see many horse trailers, tractors, farms, large manicured lawns, long property lines and fences, and huge homes.

Waterford is a throwback to country towns of the past. One of only a few National Landmark villages in the nation, Waterford was founded by Quakers in 1733. The town experienced great prosperity in the early 1800s but suffered greatly during the Civil War. Local miller Samuel Means established Virginia's only Federal force, the Loudoun Independent Rangers.

After the war, the railroad bypassed the village, and its growth stopped. But local residents began a serious renovation and restoration project in 1937, and today Waterford is a true charmer. The Waterford Foundation sponsors a three-day "Homes Tour and Crafts Exhibit" the first weekend in October, with Civil War living history, local crafts, artwork, music, dance, and tours of the many historic homes. Waterford also features nearby Loudoun Valley Vineyards. This award-winning winery offers lesser-known wines and well-known views.

Farther north, on County 665, make sure to stop in at the Taylorstown General Store. This typical country store sells almost everything and is a great provisions point for country road cyclists and drivers.

County 668 and County 672 lead on into Lovettsville. This town was originally known as the "German settlement" because it developed around its German Reformed Church in the early 1700s. Neither the Germans nor their Quaker neighbors owned slaves, so they remained loyal to the Union and even supplied men and horses to the Loudoun Independent Rangers. This small town hosted both armies coming back from the battles of Antietam and Gettysburg, but it was hard hit by the 1864 Federal burning raid.

In Lovettsville, you can tour the Porterfield Meat Store. Lovettsville also features beautiful old architecture and a variety of country stores, all framed in the scenic setting of the nearby Short Hill Mountains.

County 690 leads back south toward State 7 and another quaint country town, Hillsboro. Once the site of five mills, stately Hillsboro now features beautiful 18th- and 19th-century stone homes (many are open at Christmas) and some excellent antique shopping.

As with many towns in Loudoun County's Hunt Country, Hillsboro's citizens had mixed allegiances during the Civil War. Its strategic location also meant that both sides often passed through town. Many merchants left town, and many homes were decimated in the 1864 burning raid.

On a happier note, Susan Koerner Wright, mother of the famed Wright brothers, was born in Hillsboro. With thoughts about the sheer miracle of flight, we headed back to Purcellville, discussing the sheer miracle of a perfect country road.

If you decide to spend the night, you'll find many excellent bed-and-breakfasts in the area (see Chapter 6). One convenient favorite just south of Purcellville is the Springdale Country Inn in Lincoln. This beautiful old boarding school has been turned into a wonderful bed-and-breakfast that serves as a perfect base for exploring the area.

For More Information

Waterford Foundation: 540-882-3018

Loudoun Tourism Council: 540-771-2170

Loudoun Valley Vineyards (Waterford): 540-882-3375

Springdale Country Inn (Lincoln): 540-338-1832 or 800-388-1832

6

Days of Wine and Horses

Getting there: From Washington, take U.S. 50 west about one hour to Middleburg to begin the drive.

Highlights: Middleburg; Aldie; the Oatlands estate; Leesburg; several general stores; a stay in a bed-and-breakfast; a winery visit. This drive can easily be completed in one day, but the area deserves a weekend or more.

It's hard to believe there is so much beautiful country so close to the urban craziness of Washington, D.C. But Middleburg and the surrounding area provide the perfect country road experience for D.C. dwellers and others in the area.

The town of Middleburg is a great base for country road excursions. It was established (purchased for $2.50 an acre) in 1787 by Revolutionary War lieutenant colonel and Virginia statesman Leven Powell. It was originally called Chinn's Cross-roads, after Joseph Chinn, a first cousin of George Washington. Powell changed the name to Middleburg because of the town's location between Alexandria and Winchester along the Ashby Gap Road (now U.S. 50).

Middleburg has welcomed travelers for more than 250 years, serving as a stagecoach and resting point for early country road "drivers." Today Middleburg still welcomes travelers with open arms. The historic town offers many excellent restaurants, shops, and places to stay. The sidewalks are typically crowded with visitors exploring the quaint town on foot.

The Red Fox Inn & Tavern is my favorite place in Middleburg. It is billed as the "oldest original inn in America." During the Civil War, it served as the meeting place for Confederate colonel John Mosby and his Rangers. A hundred years later, President John F. Kennedy's press secretary Pierre Salinger held a press conference here. It now serves up great food and drink and offers wonderful rooms for those who wish to spend the night.

Some other great places to stay and eat in Middleburg include the Middleburg Country Inn, the Middleburg Inn & Guest Suites, Mosby's Tavern (for hearty fare), and the Upper Crust (for sweets). B&A Grocery can set you up with the fixings for a memorable country road picnic.

In the 20th century, Middleburg has continued to welcome guests looking for smalltown charm, good wine from local vineyards, and the horse-and-fox hunting scene. The town has a classy air and is indeed in a class of its own.

The cute little Pink Box Visitor Center, at 12 North Madison Street, can help you find other sightseeing, shopping, dining, and accommodations options. A friendly local woman, with a charming southern accent and a love of the Middleburg area, is usually on duty there.

Almost any country road out of Middleburg will work out well. We chose to explore the back roads north of town, first heading east on U.S. 50 toward Aldie. If you have time, stop by Swedenburg Estate Vineyard at Valley View Farm for a taste of Virginia wines.

The little town of Aldie was established in 1810 by Charles Fenton Mercer and was active in the Civil War. Aldie has several stores and antique shops, along with the historic

Aldie Mill, which features its original millstone hoist and is undergoing major restoration.

Just east of town, take U.S. 15 north toward Leesburg. This road passes through beautiful horse country and by large country manors, including the Oatlands estate.

Oatlands is a perfectly preserved example of a Virginia plantation and a classic Old Dominion lifestyle. The home, gardens, and 260 acres of rolling countryside are now owned by the National Trust for Historic Preservation.

The Federal-style mansion was built in 1803 by Robert "King" Carter, with bricks molded and fired on the property and wood brought from the nearby forests. The home went on to serve as a focal point for Washington and horse country social and cultural life. Today the residence features period antiques and furnishings, family memorabilia, and a large library. The beautiful gardens contain several sandstone slabs with the footprints of dinosaurs.

Two miles farther north on U.S. 15, look for the Mountain Gap School. It is one of the oldest one-room schools in the area and is now owned by the National Trust for Historic Preservation. It is open to the public.

Farther along is the city of Leesburg. It was originally called George Town, after the reigning British monarch, King George II, but broke its ties with England and changed its name to Leesburg in 1758, in honor of Virginia's Lee family.

Leesburg's Historic District listing on the National Register is cited as "one of the best preserved, most picturesque communities in Virginia." For those who know Virginia's communities, that's quite a compliment.

Leesburg is great for walking. The Loudoun Museum and Information Center at 16 West Loudoun Street is a convenient starting point. Our favorite stops included the restored log cabin next door, the Loudoun Artisan Center, Market Station, and the old Court House, where important visitors included Patrick Henry, James Monroe, and George Washington.

We also liked the southern cooking at the Laurel Brigade Inn, where we followed in the footsteps of the Marquis de Lafayette and President John Quincy Adams. For southern-style lodging, check out the Norris House Inn or the Colonial Inn.

Take State 7 out of Leesburg toward Purcellville. Compared to the road just taken and the country road to come, State 7 will seem like a busy interstate. About four miles west of Leesburg, turn left onto County 734. This short (14 miles) Virginia Byway is called the Snickersville Turnpike.

The road begins with an immediate downhill hairpin turn and never stops rolling through the countryside. The first stop is Bluemont and the Snickersville General Store. This is one of many general stores in the area, which allow nearby farmers and others to catch up on local gossip and pick up necessities without having to go into the city. The Snickersville General Store features a porch swing, fresh doughnuts, local produce, milkshakes, and a small deli.

After Bluemont, County 734 winds along through beautiful farmland. Check out the Philomont General Store and Post Office, at the corner of County 734 and County 630, before heading back to U.S. 50 and Middleburg.

This country road loop may make you thirsty, and several nearby vineyards can wet your whistle with some tasty wine. Down County 626 from Middleburg on the prerevolutionary farm of Waverly, Piedmont Vineyards provides great tours and tastings at Virginia's first commercial vinifera vineyard. In his excellent book *Parker's Wine Buyer's Guide,* Robert M. Parker Jr., says, "Virginia has one winery that produces world-class Chardonnay: The Piedmont Vineyard." Taste it yourself, right at the source.

Continue on County 626, then turn left onto County 679 and left again onto County 628. A dirt road leads to the scenic Meredyth Vineyards, one of the pioneering wineries in the booming Virginia wine industry. Owner Archie Smith offers interesting tours, award-winning wines, and a perfect setting for a picnic.

For More Information

Red Fox Inn & Tavern (Middleburg): 540-687-6301

Middleburg Country Inn: 540-687-6082

Middleburg Inn & Guest Suites: 540-587-3115 or 800-432-6125

Mosby's Tavern (Middleburg): 540-687-5282

Upper Crust (Middleburg): 540-687-5666

B&A Grocery (Middleburg): 540-687-6133

Pink Box Visitor Center (Middleburg): 540-687-8888

Swedenburg Estate Vineyard (Middleburg): 540-687-5219

Oatlands (Leesburg): 703-777-3174

Loudoun Museum and Information Center (Leesburg): 703-777-7427

Laurel Brigade Inn (Leesburg): 703-777-1010

Norris House Inn (Leesburg): 703-777-1806

Colonial Inn (Leesburg): 703-777-5000

Piedmont Vineyards (Middleburg): 540-687-5528

Meredyth Vineyards (Middleburg): 540-687-6277

7

The Valley Road

Getting there: From Washington, take I-66 west about 70 miles to I-81 or U.S. 11 and the Shenandoah Valley. The drive starts about 20 miles north of the intersection with these two routes, in Winchester. From Richmond, take I-64 west about 90 miles to I-81 or U.S. 11 and the Shenandoah Valley. The drive starts about 90 miles north of the intersection with these two routes, in Winchester. For those with limited time, this is a great starting point to explore Staunton and the southern Shenandoah Valley.

Highlights: Stunning scenery; Civil War history; quaint bed-and-breakfasts and local lodging options; wineries; excellent dining possibilities; small towns. The entire drive can be completed in one long weekend, but the Shenandoah Valley deserves many more days of exploration.

Whether it's for a weekend or a longer stay, the Shenandoah Valley offers the perfect auto tour opportunity. The location and road system make the drive a big part of the fun.

The convenience of the Shenandoah Valley is what attracts thousands of visitors annually. It is easily reached by interstate, via I-81, I-64, and I-66, and is within a one-day drive for half the population of the United States. The drive stretches 200 miles north to south, from West Virginia's Eastern Panhandle to Roanoke, Virginia.

Made famous by song and history, *Shenandoah* is an Indian word meaning "daughter of the stars." This picturesque area is flanked by wooded hills and mountains ranging in elevation from 3,000 to 5,000 feet. The "valley" is generally 10 to 20 miles wide and features many small towns and much rolling farmland.

I-81 runs the entire length of the valley, and you can follow it if you wish to make quick stops at points of interest. Historic U.S. 11 offers a slow-paced drive, with much more to see and explore along the way. The valley also features side roads leading to many small towns and tourist attractions.

This is certainly a country road for leisurely driving and lingering. It offers breathtaking scenery year-round, historical sites, world-famous caverns, renowned wineries, antique shopping, and a full array of tourist services. Accommodations range from quaint bed-and-breakfasts to large resorts. If you wish, you can use one place in the Shenandoah Valley as a base for exploration or cover the entire length for a complete overview.

"Our area is perfect for auto travel," says Andy Dawson, head of the Shenandoah Valley Travel Association. During our drive, we stopped in at the association's excellent information center in New Market for brochures and exploration ideas. "The places and the people make this a very special driving destination," Dawson adds.

Those with a lot of time may wish to explore the West Virginia portion of the Shenandoah Valley. Martinsburg offers great factory outlet shopping. To the east, history lovers will want to explore Harpers Ferry and the National Historical Battlefield Park. This town was the site of John Brown's Raid, an 1859 attempt to incite a slave revolt. Many exhibits and interpretive presentations are offered here.

The large Virginia portion of the Shenandoah Valley begins in Winchester. The town is steeped in Civil War history and the apple industry. It also is the town where I grew up.

When we came here to begin our drive, I saw things with new eyes. The town and its surrounding area provide an ideal introduction to what's down the road in the valley.

George Washington surveyed land all around Winchester in the mid-1700s and had an office here. He used this office as his headquarters during the French and Indian War.

During the Civil War, Winchester changed hands 70 times and was the scene of six big battles. Confederate forces used Winchester to cut off supplies targeted for Federal troops trying to reach Richmond. The Union army used Winchester as the beginning of a protected route down the Shenandoah Valley.

Winchester is perfect for an auto tour. The Chamber of Commerce, at 29 South Cameron Street, on U.S. 11 and U.S. 522, can provide maps and advice to start you on your way.

On Braddock Street, Confederate general Thomas "Stonewall" Jackson's Winter Headquarters feature excellent exhibits on Winchester's role in the Civil War. Jackson occupied this home from November 1861 to March 1862.

Just down the street, at the Cork Street intersection, is George Washington's Office and Headquarters. Most of the building is devoted to the history of Winchester, but one room focuses on its role in the Civil War.

You may wish to plan your visit to Winchester for the first weekend in May, when the annual Apple Blossom Festival is held. The festival features parades, fairs, and other special events. I would advise making your hotel reservations early or booking accommodations farther down U.S. 11.

U.S. 11 heads easily out of town and into the rolling hills of the Shenandoah Valley. Historic markers line the drive. Several markers cover the Civil War battles in and around Winchester.

One marker commemorates the Battle of Kernstown, which took place on March 23, 1862, when Stonewall Jackson attacked the Union forces holding Winchester. Jackson's troops were greatly outnumbered and had to withdraw south, leaving many dead soldiers on the field. The citizens of Winchester buried the soldiers after the battle. The roar of passing cars has replaced roaring cannons, but you can almost feel the history in the hills when you stop to read a marker.

Middletown is the first major stop on the drive, and it's worth major exploration. Most people head straight for the Wayside Inn for a terrific meal (and much more). This restored country inn, built in 1797, offers an excellent restaurant (try the peanut soup and other southern dishes) and 22 guest rooms furnished with antiques and private baths.

Next door is the Wayside Theatre, a popular place for seasonal theater productions. Call ahead for the schedule.

In Middletown, keep your eyes peeled for Route 11 Potato Chips, just a block off U.S. 11. Chris Miller has created a mecca for potato chip lovers in Middletown's old feed store.

You can watch as the master chip man makes the freshest and tastiest potato chips imaginable. We tasted a lot of chips and left with a big supply. Some options include seasonal Yukon Gold chips, Purple Peruvian chips, sweet potato chips, and mixed root vegetable chips (for instance, taro root, beet, parsnip, and carrot chips).

You can purchase 11-ounce "personal munch" bags, one-and-a-half-pound "gift-giving" tins, or three-pound "let's party" bags. Miller offers shipping by phone or fax, but be sure to stop by for a visit and snack.

Just south of Middletown is Belle Grove Plantation. The stunning house was built in 1794 by Maj. Isaac Hite Jr. His grandfather, Jost Hite, was one of the first permanent settlers in the Shenandoah Valley.

The house is architecturally significant because of the active involvement of Thomas Jefferson in its design. Jefferson's help was solicited by his friend, James Madison, whose sister married Major Hite.

Madison wrote to Jefferson in October 1794, explaining, "This letter will be handed to you by Mr. Bond who is to build a large house for Mr. Hite my brother-in-law on my suggestion he is to visit Monticello not only to profit of examples before his eyes, but to ask the favor of your advice on the plan of the house." Jefferson's influence can immediately be seen in the "pavilion style" architecture.

Belle Grove played an important role in the Battle of Cedar Creek in October 1864. This battle was fought by troops under Union general Philip Sheridan and Confederate general Jubal Early.

Early's troops attacked the sleeping Union army encamped around General Sheridan's headquarters at Belle Grove. They routed the Union troops before Sheridan could return from a War Department conference in Washington.

When news of the battle reached Sheridan in Winchester, he made his famous "ride to the front"—a ride immortalized in a poem by Thomas Buchanan Read. Sheridan regained control of the valley, which the Union would retain for the rest of the war.

Along with excellent tours of the house and grounds, Belle Grove offers all sorts of seasonal activities. Ask about the Needlework Exhibition, Shenandoah Valley Farm Craft Days, Musical Feast, and Christmas at Belle Grove.

Just 10 minutes down the road is Strasburg, rightfully known as "The Antique Capital of the Blue Ridge." The Strasburg Emporium will delight antique shoppers, with

almost 100 dealers under one roof. The 65,000-square-foot building offers country and formal furniture, folk and fine art, and a wide variety of collectibles. Strasburg also features several other antique shops.

The Strasburg Museum, located in an old steam pottery and train depot, provides an overview of the history of Strasburg and the Shenandoah Valley. Displays cover pottery, farming, Native Americans, local life, and the Civil War. Have someone at the museum explain the "Great Train Raid of 1861." This incredible feat by Stonewall Jackson, more than 200 men, and a lot of horses involved the physical movement of trains and heavy fighting equipment from Harpers Ferry to Strasburg (it took four days). The museum displays a large barrel-rifling machine thought to be one of the few remaining pieces of arms-making equipment moved by Jackson.

Just north of town on U.S. 11, the Hupp's Hill Battlefield Park and Study Center is a Civil War museum dedicated to teaching people (especially children) through hands-on exhibits. Shenandoah Valley native Todd Kern offers interesting insight into the Civil War. The museum features a mural detailing the history of the Civil War, the world's largest map of the Battle of Cedar Creek, and the world's third largest collection of Confederate currency.

Strasburg also offers a great place to stop for the night: the Hotel Strasburg. This old hospital has been completely restored to retain the Victorian elegance of the 1890s.

Gary Rutherford has made the Hotel Strasburg a respite for many visitors. He offers wonderful rooms (unoccupied rooms are open for all to explore), a superb little bar, and excellent regional cooking. As much as we love driving, we hated to leave this hotel.

East of Strasburg, near Front Royal, is the entrance to Shenandoah National Park and the Skyline Drive (see Chapter 8).

The park features more than 370 miles of trails in the heart of the Blue Ridge Mountains. The Skyline Drive meanders along the ridge of the park for 105 miles, featuring stunning views and many accommodations options along the way. This road is one of the finest drives in the United States and can be accessed at several points.

Back in the heart of the valley, friendly towns such as Woodstock, Edinburg, and Mount Jackson are perfect places to stop for a look at local Shenandoah Valley life, past and present.

In Woodstock, look for the oldest county courthouse (1792) in use west of the Blue Ridge Mountains. Overnighters should head for the Inn at Narrow Passage. This log inn overlooking the Shenandoah River has been welcoming travelers since the early 1740s. It was a haven for settlers on the Virginia frontier, a stagecoach inn on the old Valley Turnpike, and the 1862 headquarters for Stonewall Jackson during the Valley Campaign.

Ellen and Ed Markel now welcome visitors to this quaint bed-and-breakfast, which is furnished with antiques and handcrafted colonial reproductions. They offer comfortable rooms with private or shared baths. Some of the rooms have romantic and rustic wood-burning fireplaces and canopied beds.

The Markels love to share the Shenandoah Valley with visitors. They serve a hearty breakfast in a charming colonial dining room, where a cheery fire warms the room in cool weather. The living room, with its massive limestone fireplace, is a cozy meeting place. In warm weather, the porches overlooking the sloping lawns and river are perfect places to plan valley explorations.

Heading south out of Woodstock, look for Shenandoah Vineyards, which you reach by turning right onto County 605 and then left onto County 686. Owner Emma Randel has made

Shenandoah Vineyards one of the state's most renowned wineries. We loved our long visit. The winery and vineyards are open year-round. They offer an informative self-guided tour and educational and enjoyable wine tastings. Shenandoah Vineyards has won many awards, and the wine tasting will lure you into buying bottles to take home. We particularly liked the Shenandoah Blanc. The active vineyard features an annual harvest festival, a pig roast, and many other events.

Back on U.S. 11 in Edinburg, fishing fanatics will want to stop by Murray's Fly Shop, located inside the town pharmacy at 211 Main Street. Murray is a nationally known fisherman who has written several successful books and runs popular fly-fishing schools. Call first to see if he is there.

In Mount Jackson, many people head for the mountains and Bryce Resort. This four-season resort offers skiing, golf, tennis, boating, and a variety of accommodations. In warmer weather, call ahead to see if the popular Shenandoah Valley Music Festival is taking place. The festival is held outdoors in Orkney Springs.

Just south of Mount Jackson, look for the turn to the covered bridge, on County 720. This is the longest covered bridge of the nine remaining in Virginia and is the only one across the Shenandoah River. It was built in 1893 and stretches 191 feet across the river in a single span.

If you've never visited underground caverns, the Shenandoah Valley is the place to start. If you've already seen some caverns, go anyway. Shenandoah Caverns are convenient to U.S. 11 and provide an ideal introduction to the underbelly of the Shenandoah Valley (it's even pretty underground).

Follow the signs from U.S. 11 to the other side of I-81. You might want to make a quick pit stop at the Tuttle & Spice

General Store. This old-fashioned gift shop is a step back in time to the 1880s, with sweets, local food items, crafts, and much more. The Village Museum features an old-time general store, soda parlor, toy store, and tobacco shop. Shenandoah Caverns surprise many people with their beauty and stunning lighting. You descend by elevator to Bacon Hall, where the formations look like strips of bacon. This sets the tone for the rest of the mile-long walking tour.

Some of our favorite formations include the Capitol Dome in Cathedral Hall (it looks like the U.S. Capitol) and Rainbow Lake (beautiful reflections in a shallow pond). The lighting allows for some great picture-taking possibilities.

In New Market, most people head straight for the battlefield, but two shops in town on U.S. 11 are worth a stop. The Christmas Gallery is a year-round Christmas shop, offering memorable Shenandoah Valley souvenirs. Nearby, check out the Bedrooms of America Museum & Pottery, with 11 rooms furnished with authentic furniture from around 1650 to around 1930.

We enjoyed some tasty cooking at the Southern Kitchen. The restaurant has been in the Newland family since 1955 and serves good food at reasonable prices. We lingered over dessert and coffee, planning our New Market Battlefield visit.

The New Market area played a key role in the Civil War. The New Market Battlefield Historical Park memorializes the brave charge of cadets from the Virginia Military Institute (VMI) on May 15, 1864.

This was a nostalgic trip for me. I graduated from VMI and can still remember memorizing the names of the 10 cadets who died at New Market (as part of the harsh initiation period of freshmen "Rats" at the legendary school).

In the spring of 1864, Lt. Gen. Ulysses S. Grant decided to take control of the strategically important and agriculturally rich Shenandoah Valley and to press the Confederacy into submission. Grant sent an army of 10,000 Union soldiers to secure the valley and threaten the left flank of Robert E. Lee's forces. In response, Confederate Gen. John C. Breckinridge was able to muster a force of just 4,500 troops. They were joined by 247 eager cadets from VMI, who marched north from Lexington.

General Breckinridge decided to force the battle on the morning of May 15, saying, "We can attack and whip them here and I'll do it." The bloody fighting raged for hours, and Breckinridge was forced to use the VMI cadets. They helped to rally the troops and contributed to a major Confederate victory. This was the only time in history that an American cadet corp has ever participated in pitched battle.

We enjoyed exploring the extensive background exhibits at the park and taking a walking tour of the area. The Hall of Valor Museum is a monument to the VMI Corps of Cadets and all American Civil War soldiers. Also offered is a comprehensive and nonpartisan survey of major Civil War events, as well as two excellent films, *New Market—A Field of Honor* and *Stonewall's Valley*.

The walking tour allowed us to follow the action of the VMI cadets in the battle. The walk leads over the rolling hills to a restored farmhouse in the center of the action, the "Field of Lost Shoes," and high bluffs 200 feet above the Shenandoah River.

Civil War buffs also will want to visit the nearby New Market Battlefield Military Museum. This newer museum features one of the largest collections of historically important memorabilia pertaining to the Civil War, the Battle of New Market, and U.S. military history.

The Shenandoah Valley Travel Association Information Center is located near the turn for the New Market Battlefield Historical Park. Open daily from 9:00 A.M. to 5:00 P.M., this is a great place to pick up information and literature about the entire Shenandoah Valley.

East of New Market, Luray draws many visitors to its historic streets and colorful caverns. The town is a great base for exploring the mountains of Shenandoah National Park and along the Skyline Drive.

Luray and surrounding Page County offer great backroad driving. The Chamber of Commerce at 6 East Main Street has information on four self-guided tours of the area.

When we stopped by, the person on duty told us about some of the unusual homes nearby. When this area was part of the American frontier, attack by Indians was a constant concern. Many families built small "forts" for protection. These "forts" were usually in the basement and contained food, water, and a fireplace. These home fortresses are now farm residences, but visitors are usually welcome. The Chamber of Commerce can help with visits to the Egypt House, Fort Paul Long, Fort Rhodes, the Shirley Home, Fort Song, and Fort Stover.

Luray also lures many people to Luray Caverns. This large facility features a one-hour tour along paved walkways. Luray Caverns include the world's only "stalacpipe" organ, which features stalactites being struck by electronically controlled rubber-tipped plungers. The result is music of symphonic quality. Other highlights include 140-foot-high ceilings, a crystal-clear wishing well, and formations resembling fried eggs, sunny-side up.

The drive from New Market to Harrisonburg features farmland and history. Harrisonburg is the home of James Madison University and Eastern Mennonite College, as well as the headquarters for the George Washington National Forest (the mountainous western boundary of the Shenandoah Valley).

The highlight for us was the Joshua Wilton House. This restored 1888 Victorian home at 412 South Main Street is one of the Shenandoah Valley's most elegant lodging and dining possibilities. Craig and Roberta Moore spoil their guests, whether they're there just for dinner or for a longer stay.

The five modern guest rooms are charming. A wonderful bar offers visitors a great way to meet like-minded travelers and locals. The Moores' chef serves creative dishes in three dining rooms, in the sun room, and on an outdoor terrace. For a more casual atmosphere, go to JM's, just down the street from the Joshua Wilton House. Another great spot is Spanky's, a small Virginia chain of restaurants offering unusual sandwiches and a friendly atmosphere.

The drive to Staunton is short and sweet. This scenic city is one of the valley's most varied stops. It offers great shopping, dining, and accommodations and deserves more than a brief visit.

One of our true finds in Staunton was the Belle Grae Inn. We were greeted by Bell Boy, the resident dog. After a quick tour of the grounds, we decided to stay.

Innkeeper Michael Organ has created a lodging and dining masterpiece. He started in 1983 by restoring the main house (now referred to as the Old Inn). Since then, he has completed renovations on a variety of small Victorian houses bordering the property. The result is a blend of many accommodations options. Our favorites include the Jefferson House, the Townhouse, and the Bishop's Suite, but anything he has available is wonderful. The food matches the atmosphere, with romantic dining in the Old Inn or more casual fare in the café.

When the Belle Grae Inn is full, Michael sends visitors to the Sampson Eagon Inn or the Frederick House. We stopped by both and hope to return soon. Frank and Laura Mattingly run the Sampson Eagon Inn, an antebellum mansion in the heart of town. Joe and Evy Harman are the innkeepers at the Frederick House, a small European-style hotel downtown.

Michael gave us plenty of tips for exploring the Staunton area. He owns an eclectic men's shop in town, called Rails. It's just one of several interesting shopping opportunities. Ask Michael (or almost anyone else) for a shopping brochure.

We stopped by the Staunton Office of Tourism (116 West Beverley Street) for tips on exploring the city. The Woodrow Wilson Birthplace & Museum gives a great overview of the life of our 28th president. My favorite exhibit was President Wilson's Pierce-Arrow limousine.

The other mecca in Staunton is the Statler Brothers Complex at 501 Thornrose Avenue. The Statlers are from Staunton, and this mini-museum features exhibits on their lives and a souvenir shop.

The surrounding countryside offers many great outings (the Belle Grae Inn has a brochure). One of the most fascinating is the Museum of American Frontier Culture. This hugely successful undertaking features 18th- and 19th-century working farms from England, Germany, Ireland, and the United States. The museum provides a great overview of the development of the Shenandoah Valley.

The hilly drive down U.S. 11 from Staunton to Lexington is filled with fertile farmland. Twenty miles south of Staunton, look for the turnoff to the Cyrus McCormick Memorial Museum. It was here that McCormick perfected the grain reaper in 1831 and changed the face of farming forever. The mill building features interesting exhibits and is open only during warm-weather months.

A few more miles south, we spent a wonderful night at the Oak Spring Farm Bed & Breakfast, located just off U.S. 11 in Raphine. It is owned and operated by Frank and Sandy Harrelson. They offer four modern rooms, each with a private bath. Their beautiful 1826 plantation manor house is on the National Historical Registry and is a Virginia Historical Landmark. It is impressively furnished with antiques and family heirlooms.

Frank and Sandy run a professional bed-and-breakfast operation. They take great pride in making their guests feel at home and offer a full gourmet southern breakfast. They add a lot of little touches that make a big difference to their many repeat guests. We really enjoyed roaming the grounds, which include a large orchard, a pasture area with an ever-changing cast of miniature farm animals from the Natural Bridge Zoo, and extensive lawns and gardens.

The large, red barn that greets you as you turn down the road to their house is a landmark to people in Rockbridge County. During the Civil War the barn had a blacksmith shop which was being used to shoe horses for the Southern army. Gen. David Hunter was dispatched by Gen. Phillip Sheridan to capture and burn the Virginia Military Institute in Lexington. On his way to Lexington, marching down the Valley Turnpike, he burned the barn, but fortunately spared the house. The barn was rebuilt after the war in March 1881. Still structurally sound, it continues to be used today as a working barn.

The many farm and Indian relics found buried on the grounds and in the attic of the house will intrigue any visitor to the home.

Just a few miles south, Lexington lures travelers with historical and modern-day attractions. A 19th-century college town, Lexington is home to both VMI and Washington and Lee University.

Because I graduated from VMI, that was our first stop in Lexington. VMI was founded in 1839 and is the oldest state-supported military college in the nation. It is called "The West Point of the South." Stonewall Jackson taught at VMI, and the distinguished list of citizen-soldier graduates includes Gen. George C. Marshall.

We strolled the stark campus as I recalled the good (and bad) times I had during my four years here. Highlights include the cadet barracks, the VMI Chapel and Museum, the George C. Marshall Research Museum, and the dress parades often held on Fridays or Saturdays.

Washington and Lee University, right next door, was

founded in 1749. Originally named Washington University upon its endowment by George Washington in 1749, the university added the name Lee after Robert E. Lee's death in 1870. (Lee served as college president following the Civil War and helped build up the enrollment.)

Less foreboding than VMI, the grounds at Washington and Lee are gorgeous. Make sure to go into Lee Chapel, where Lee is buried.

In town, start your tour at the Lexington Visitors Bureau and Visitor Center. This modern facility features several displays and much information, and someone there can give you a plan for touring the town.

Our favorite stops (all within walking distance) include the Stonewall Jackson House, Jackson's pre–Civil War home; the Stonewall Jackson Memorial Cemetery, with much more than his grave; and the Lexington Carriage Company, for narrated carriage rides through Lexington's downtown and residential districts. Our other favorite stop in the area is Spanky's for great sandwiches.

Just 14 miles south of Lexington is Natural Bridge, one of the seven natural wonders of the world. This 215-foot-high stone arch was carved by water over the centuries and stands as one of the Shenandoah Valley's most famous sites.

George Washington surveyed this land in 1750 and carved his initials in the archway. Each night, a colorful presentation called "The Drama of Creation" is performed at Natural Bridge. The Natural Bridge Wax Museum next door includes well-done figures from folklore and regional personalities.

The area south to Roanoke is fairly uneventful compared to the rest of the Shenandoah Valley. You even have to get on the interstate (sorry) for about 10 miles, but once you get to Roanoke, you'll be glad you made the trip.

Roanoke is the valley's largest city. It is known as the "Star City of the South," symbolized by a huge neon star on

The Natural Bridge in Shenandoah Valley

Mill Mountain overlooking the city. Roanoke and the surrounding valley is the perfect place to end a country road drive.

This city is justifiably famous for its Historic Farmers Market, where farmers have been selling their fresh fruits, vegetables, and flowers for nearly 120 years. It is generally open every day except Sundays and is full of refreshing sights, sounds, and smells. The flavor of the market is enhanced by the restored City Market Building and its international food court, as well as the nearly 100 lively shops, antique dealers, art galleries, and restaurants that surround the produce stalls.

Roanoke's other pride and joy is Center in the Square, a multicultural complex with several facets. The Science Museum of Western Virginia teaches the wonders of science through hands-on exhibits. The Roanoke Museum of Fine Arts features the works of local, regional, and international artists. Mill Mountain Theatre offers professional and alternative productions on a regular basis.

Our favorite stop in Center in the Square was the Roanoke Valley History Museum, which contains artifacts from the area's prehistoric period, through frontier settlement and the boom days of the railroad, and up to the present. The newest permanent exhibit is "To the Rescue," which honors Roanoke as the birthplace of the international volunteer rescue squad movement.

The rest of downtown Roanoke is great for walking. Highlights of our weekend there included the fascinating Virginia Museum of Transportation (dozens of big trains and other vehicles) and the Harrison Museum of African American Culture. Just outside town, we found the Epperly family's Miniature Graceland (you have to see it to believe it).

Some favorite food stops include Carlos Brazilian International Cuisine, Corned Beef and Company, the Lone Star Cantina and Brewery, and Mill Mountain Coffee & Tea. To sleep, check into the well-known Patrick Henry Hotel.

The city's most popular man-made attraction is the neon star on Mill Mountain. The 88-foot-high lighted star has 2,000 feet of neon tubing that can be seen on a clear night for a 60-mile radius. Nearby is Mill Mountain Zoological Park, a fun little park for endangered species.

Mill Mountain is up near the Blue Ridge Parkway (see Chapter 9) and offers a spectacular view of Roanoke and the Shenandoah Valley. From there you can see U.S. 11, the valley's perfect country road, making its way north to Winchester.

For More Information

Harpers Ferry and the National Historical Battlefield Park (Harpers Ferry, WV): 304-535-6371

Winchester Chamber of Commerce: 540-662-4118 or 800-662-1360

Wayside Inn (Middletown): 540-869-1797

Wayside Theatre (Middletown): 540-869-1776

Route 11 Potato Chips (Middletown): 540-869-0104

Belle Grove Plantation (Middletown): 540-869-2028

Strasburg Emporium: 540-465-3711

Hupp's Hill Battlefield Park and Study Center (Strasburg): 540-465-5884

Hotel Strasburg: 540-465-9191 or 800-348-8327

Inn at Narrow Passage (Woodstock): 540-459-8000

Shenandoah Vineyards (Edinburg): 540-984-8699

Murray's Fly Shop (Edinburg): 540-984-4212

Bryce Resort (Basye): 540-856-2121

Shenandoah Caverns: 540-477-3115

Southern Kitchen (New Market): 540-740-3514

New Market Battlefield Historical Park: 540-740-3101

New Market Battlefield Military Museum: 540-740-8065

Shenandoah Valley Travel Association Information Center (New Market): 540-740-3132

Luray Caverns: 540-743-6551

Joshua Wilton House (Harrisonburg): 540-434-4464

Staunton/Augusta Travel Information Center (Staunton): 540-332-3865

Belle Grae Inn (Staunton): 540-886-5151

Sampson Eagon Inn (Staunton): 540-886-2200

Frederick House (Staunton): 540-885-4220 or 800-334-5575

Staunton Office of Tourism: 540-332-3865

Statler Brothers Complex (Staunton): 540-885-7297

Museum of American Frontier Culture (Staunton): 540-332-7850

Cyrus McCormick Memorial Museum (Steeles Tavern): 540-377-2255

Oak Spring Farm Bed and Breakfast (Lexington): 540-377-2398

Lexington Visitors Bureau and Visitor Center:
 540-463-3777

Natural Bridge: 540-291-2121 or 800-533-1410

Natural Bridge Wax Museum: 540-291-2426

Roanoke Valley Visitor Information Center: 540-345-8622

Patrick Henry Hotel (Roanoke): 540-345-8811

8

The Skyline Drive

Getting there: From Washington, take I-66 west about an hour to Front Royal. Take the Skyline Drive exit and follow the signs for about a mile to the entrance to the drive.

Highlights: Beautiful overlooks; hiking trails; horseback riding; Appalachian Trail; Dickey Ridge Visitor Center; Skyland; Hawksbill Mountain summit; Big Meadows; Loft Mountain. This drive can be completed in one day, but this doesn't allow time for hiking or camping. At least a long weekend is recommended.

The Skyline Drive is one of the nation's most beautiful stretches of road. But budget-balancing measures have taken their toll on the national park system, and the Skyline Drive has not been immune to these cuts. Although the drive now has fewer options to pursue, we found ourselves spending more time exploring its simpler pleasures. Just make sure you call ahead to confirm schedules and availability.

The two-lane Skyline Drive runs along a beautiful part of the Blue Ridge Mountains and Shenandoah National Park, which make up the eastern section of the Appalachian Mountains. Most of the rocks that form the mountains are part of volcanic formations more than one billion years old. The area has been inhabited by humans for about 9,000 years, with primitive food gatherers and Native Americans as early residents.

After the Shenandoah Valley was settled, farmers moved into the mountains for more farmland. Slowly but surely, the soil, forests, and wildlife started to disappear.

Congress authorized the establishment of Shenandoah National Park in 1926. More than half the area's inhabitants had already left the mountains, and the remaining residents either sold their land or were relocated with government help. The state bought almost 260 square miles of land and donated it to the federal government.

In a massive undertaking, the Civilian Conservation Corps built recreational facilities during the 1930s, and the Skyline Drive was completed in 1939. The area was allowed to return to its natural state, and now more than 95 percent of the park is covered by forests.

In the words of Shenandoah National Park Superintendent J. W. Wade, "What makes Shenandoah a sanctuary for its ecosystems makes the park a sanctuary for humans, too." The Skyline Drive offers the perfect way to explore this natural beauty. It runs 105 miles from the north entrance at Front Royal to the south entrance at Rockfish Gap. The speed limit is a leisurely 35 MPH, and the road is marked by excellent signs, concrete mile markers, and rock fence guardrails.

Wildlife abounds, including deer, bears, bobcats, turkeys, and many other animals. It's possible that you'll see a bear or a bobcat, but it's more likely that you'll see some of the 200 species of birds, deer, and smaller animals that inhabit the area.

This country road is beautiful during any season. Spring brings berries, wildflowers, and beautiful red maple buds. Many animals, such as groundhogs and chipmunks, can be seen.

Summer comes quickly, with deep greens covering the mountains at a rate of 100 feet in elevation each day. The warm weather brings more wildflowers, lots of chirping birds, and shy fawns.

The fall colors attract leaf peepers, so it's best to plan a drive during the week if possible. The colors typically reach their peak in mid-October, but a quick phone call will confirm this.

Most facilities along the Skyline Drive close November 1, but the road remains open. This makes for super views during the winter. The road is, however, closed during bad weather.

The natural beauty of the drive begins almost immediately. South of Front Royal, you pay $5.00 per car for the privilege of driving along one of the nation's premier country roads. The entrance station is staffed by friendly National Park Service personnel, who can answer questions and provide specific recommendations.

The entire drive is blessed with beautiful overlooks, and drivers are frequently drawn off the road for some spectacular views. Stop often and look for great hiking, picnicking, and sightseeing spots.

The first major pulloff is the Shenandoah Valley Overlook, which provides a wide view of the valley across to Signal Knob, a Civil War communications post up on Massanutten Mountain in the distance. This pretty mountain divides the Shenandoah Valley and the Shenandoah River, with the north fork of the river on the far side. The two forks meet north of Front Royal.

At milepost 4.6, the Dickey Ridge Visitor Center is a perfect place to stop for information and touring ideas. We often stop there to check times for ranger talks and walks, hiking recommendations, and what's open and closed. This major facility features exhibits on Skyline Drive services and activities, an interesting sales outlet, park rangers to answer questions, a self-guided nature trail, and much more.

The drive continues south, with many more overlooks and views. Our favorite pulloffs include Gooney Run, Range View, and Hogback Overlook, which offer great views of several of the bends in the Shenandoah River.

Matthews Arm Campground at milepost 22.2 is the first of many accommodations options along the Skyline Drive. (Due to budget constraints, it has been closed temporarily.) This campground features tent and trailer sites, excellent hiking trails, and many ranger-led hikes and campfire programs. Just down the road, picnicking is available at Elkwallow, and great hiking (with access to the Appalachian Trail) is found at Beahms Gap (milepost 28.5).

Milepost 31.5 features another popular entrance to the Skyline Drive, with U.S. 211 from Warrenton to Luray passing through Thornton Gap. If you're hungry, the Panorama restaurant offers good food and great views. Shenandoah National Park headquarters is four miles west of the Skyline Drive on U.S. 211.

About a mile past Thornton Gap is Marys Rock Tunnel. This car tunnel, built in 1932, passes through 600 feet of rock with a 13-foot clearance. Some fun picture possibilities are available at both ends.

At Skyland (mileposts 41.7 and 42.5), one of the busiest spots on the drive, you'll find information, food, and accommodations. At 3,680 feet, it is the highest point on the drive.

Naturalist George Freeman Pollock, a major backer of the park, built Skyland in the 1890s. Today it is a popular destination for many Skyline Drive visitors. The Appalachian Trail also runs right through it.

The Skyland Lodge features large rooms with terraces overlooking the Shenandoah Valley. Several rustic cabins also are available for rent. In addition, Skyland has a spacious restaurant with great views.

The surrounding area offers much to explore, including the Stony Man Nature Trail (1.5 miles), many ranger-led walks and programs, and horseback riding.

Just down the road are two pulloffs for the hike to Hawksbill Mountain summit, which at 4,051 feet is the highest point in Shenandoah National Park. We like stopping at the Upper Hawksbill Parking Area (milepost 46.7) for the pleasant two-mile round-trip trek.

The Big Meadows area (mileposts 51 and 51.2) is an unusual sight to behold. Park managers have intentionally kept it open to show how the area looked before vegetative regeneration.

This busy area also is a great place for a short or long stop. A large number of services and activities are offered at three sites connected by roads and trails.

The best place to start a Big Meadows stop is at the Byrd Visitor Center, where rangers can help with plans, information, hikes, and much more. The wayside facilities nearby include a coffee shop, camp store, gift shop, and service station (there aren't too many on the Skyline Drive, so watch your tank).

The Big Meadows Lodge features spacious rooms and cabins overlooking the Shenandoah Valley. Camping (no trailer hookups) is very popular at Big Meadows, so call ahead for reservations. Big Meadows also has a casually rustic restaurant with great views.

South of Big Meadows, the Bearfence Mountain pulloff at milepost 56.4 makes for a great short hike. The summit is less than a half mile from the parking area, but part of it is more of a rock scramble than a standard hike. The effort is worth it, though, because Bearfence Mountain provides a 360-degree view.

Just a mile farther on, Lewis Mountain provides another

place to eat, sleep, and be merry in the great outdoors. Camping and cabin accommodations, as well as a camp store, picnicking, and campground programs, are available.

Swift Run Gap at milepost 65.7 is another major entrance to the park. It's a great starting point if you wish to cover only part of the drive. U.S. 33 crosses the Skyline Drive at this point. The Loft Mountain Campground at milepost 79.5 offers a host of facilities and activities. This area features popular hiking trails, ranger-led hikes, and campfire programs in the summer.

At milepost 84.1, you can park at Jones Run while you make the 3.6-mile round-trip hike to Jones Run Falls. This 42-foot falls features bright green mosses and flowering plants growing all along the water-sprayed cliff. It's a great place to cool off in the summer and to find some peace and quiet in the off-season.

Milepost 105.4 marks the end of the Skyline Drive. The Blue Ridge Parkway (see Chapter 9) is straight ahead, making this country road duo one of the best "no-turn" drives in the world.

For More Information

Potomac Appalachian Trail Club (Vienna): 703-242-0315

Shenandoah Natural History Association (Luray): 540-999-3582

Shenandoah National Park (Luray): 540-999-2266 (recorded message); 540-743-5108 or 800-999-4714 (lodging reservations); 800-732-0911 (emergency only)

Shenandoah Valley Travel Association Information Center (New Market): 540-740-3132

Skyland Stables, Skyline Drive: 540-999-2210 (horseback-riding reservations)

9

Virginia's Blue Ridge Parkway

Getting there: From Richmond, take I-64 west past Charlottesville to the Rockfish Gap and Blue Ridge Parkway exit. Head south on the Blue Ridge Parkway to start the drive. The facilities at this entrance offer a perfect opportunity to get gas and provisions, which are limited along the drive.

Highlights: Incredible views; leisurely driving and pulloffs; Peaks of Otter; Mabry Mill.

The Blue Ridge Parkway offers one of the ultimate country road drives. It meets all the prerequisites in resounding fashion: just two lanes; historical interest; friendly and interesting people; great scenery; good food and accommodations. What more could you ask of a country road?

Since its inception, the Blue Ridge Parkway has been called America's favorite drive. It was authorized in the 1930s as a public-works project but was half a century in the making. It was the nation's first (and ultimately longest) rural parkway. It connects Shenandoah National Park in Virginia (the Skyline Drive) with Great Smoky Mountains National

67

Park in North Carolina. Virginia's portion features about 215 miles of pure country road pleasure.

Before driving onto the parkway, many visitors make a pilgrimage to the P. Buckley Moss Museum in Waynesboro (just down I-64 west at U.S. 340 south). Moss is an internationally known artist who has a unique style often depicting country life. Many of her works are exhibited here, and the museum has an excellent gift shop.

The Blue Ridge Parkway officially starts at Rockfish Gap, where you find the zero milepost marker. These markers will inform you of your location throughout the drive.

The first major stop is indicative of what the drive has to offer. The Humpback Rocks Visitor Center (milepost 5.9) is often the first taste of the Blue Ridge Parkway for southbound drivers, and it's breathtaking.

The visitors centers, camping facilities, and concessions along the parkway are excellent, with services varying with the season. These facilities are great places to get maps, ask questions, and learn about campfire talks, nature walks, slide shows, and more.

The Humpback Rocks area features an interesting self-guided tour through a reconstructed mountain farmstead. The short (three-quarters of a mile), steep hike up to Humpback Rocks (at milepost 6.1) is well worth the effort.

Just down the road is the turnoff for Wintergreen Resort, a thriving four-season mountain resort offering skiing, golf, tennis, swimming, an equestrian center, an indoor spa, accommodations, and restaurants. It's a great place to stay if you get a late start on the parkway.

Country road fans will want to head for the Trillium House, a country inn run by Ed and Betty Dinwiddie since 1983. The Dinwiddies offer 12 quaint guest rooms, a spacious "great room" (perfect for après-ski and après-hike chats), a popular TV room, and an interesting family library. Meals are served in the dining room (with wonderful views of the mountain and golf course). Breakfasts are huge, and weekend meals are worth a drive down (or up) the mountain.

Back on the Blue Ridge Parkway, the views begin. If you stopped for every awe-inspiring view, you'd never make it to the North Carolina border. There are pulloffs at most of the better overlooks, but you're also allowed to pull over onto the shoulder as long as your car is completely off the road. The speed limit is 45 MPH or less. Wooden guardrails protect cars (and people) from the steep drop-offs.

Some possible stops along this stretch include Ravens Roost (milepost 10.7), featuring vistas of the Shenandoah River and Torry Mountain; Sherando Lake (take County 814 at milepost 16 for 4.5 miles), a recreational lake in the George Washington National Forest; Whetstone Ridge, which provided mountain folks with a fine-grained sharpening stone; and Yankee Horse Parking Area, where a hard-riding Union soldier's horse supposedly fell and had to be shot (there's now a reconstructed spur of an old logging railroad).

For a pleasant diversion, take U.S. 60 west and then left on U.S. 501 for a couple of blocks, where curious country store lovers will find The General Store, a historic general store established in 1891.

Between mileposts 58 and 64, Otter Creek runs down the Blue Ridge Parkway, following the road to the James River. Otters don't play along the creek anymore, but a lot of people do. This section of the drive features a year-round campground, visitors center, self-guided nature trail, restored lock and canal system, restaurant, and gift shop, as well as the lowest elevation on the parkway (649 feet).

A long climb gets you back into the clouds on Apple Orchard Mountain. The mountain peaks at 4,229 feet; the parkway is at 3,950 feet, its highest point in Virginia. At milepost 83.8, Wilkinson Gap offers a great hiking opportunity into Fallingwater Cascades. This hike, which follows the flow of Fallingwater Creek, is a nice 1.5-mile loop.

Peaks of Otter is one of the highlights of the drive. Stop for a few hours, the night, or a few days. Peaks of Otter Lodge is a great way to enjoy life along the parkway. The lodge offers simple rooms overlooking Abbott Lake. The restaurant features superb dining, with a special "Buffet from the Sea" on Friday nights and a "Country Dinner Buffet" on Sunday nights.

The Peaks of Otter area also has some great hiking. Head to the visitors center for a detailed map and information from the friendly staff (it must be the mountain air). Some good bets are Sharp Top Trail (1.6 steep miles for a 360-degree view); easy Elk Run Loop Trail; strenuous Harkening Hill Loop Trail; Johnson Farm Trail; and Flat Top Trail back to Fallingwater Cascades.

As you continue south on the parkway, look for the Appalachian Trail Overlook around milepost 100. The famed Appalachian Trail is a 2,100-mile hiking "path" along the ridge of the Appalachian Mountains, stretching from Maine to Georgia. It runs through 14 states, and the Virginia section (534 miles) is the longest stretch.

Benton MacKaye of Shirley Center, Massachusetts, was the first to come up with the long trail idea. It started in New Jersey in 1922. Arthur Perkins and Myron H. Avery made MacKaye's dream a reality by working with government agencies (such as the Civilian Conservation Corps) and thousands of volunteers to complete the trail.

Roanoke is situated very close to the Blue Ridge Parkway and can serve as an ideal stopover. Other quaint stopover towns include Waynesboro, Lexington, Lynchburg, and Galax.

Back along the spine of the Blue Ridge, stop at Pine Spur Parking Overlook (milepost 144.8) for an ode to the white pine, the tree depicted on the parkway emblem. Just past milepost 154, Smart View offers 500 acres of hiking trails and the former cabin home of T. T. Trail, a local mountain man.

Smalltown fans should make the short side trip to Floyd, six miles north of the parkway via State 8, just past milepost 165. Floyd features the Pine Tavern Lodge & Restaurant (established in 1927), home cooking at the Blue Ridge Restaurant, and year-round Christmas shopping at the Country Christmas House (formerly the Possum Hollow School House).

Like Peaks of Otter, the Rocky Knob area is one of the highlights of the drive. The visitors center has some spectacular hiking recommendations and information about accommodations in the Rocky Knob Cabins, a memorable way to spend the night in the Blue Ridge Mountains.

Mabry Mill is just down the road. This often-photographed water-powered mill was operated by E. B. Mabry from 1910 to 1935. The self-guided walking tour includes his gristmill, sawmill, and blacksmith shop, as well as other outdoor exhibits. In the summer and fall, visitors will often find old-time skills being demonstrated.

Nearby, the Mabry Mill Coffee & Craft Shop offers refreshments and stone-ground cornmeal. Just down the Parkway, Meadows of Dan provides gas, food, lodging, and shopping. The Hilltop Restaurant has been offering country cooking since 1952, with a great buffet, lots of locals (always a sign of good food), and friendly waitresses.

Along the rest of the Virginia portion of the Blue Ridge Parkway, check out the Groundhog Mountain Parking Overlook, with an observation tower simulating an old tobacco barn; the quaint town of Fancy Gap; and Puckett Cabin, the home of Orelena Hawks Puckett, a legendary local midwife.

With apologies to the great state of North Carolina, we hated to see the end of one of America's best country road drives.

For More Information

P. Buckley Moss Museum (Waynesboro): 540-949-6473

Blue Ridge Parkway, 2551 Mountain Road, Vinton, VA 24179:
   540-857-2213

Wintergreen Resort: 804-325-2200

Trillium House (Wintergreen): 804-325-9126 or 800-325-9126

The General Store (Buena Vista): 540-261-3860

Peaks of Otter Lodge (Bedford): 540-586-1081

Appalachian Trail Conference, P.O. Box 807, Harpers Ferry,
   WV 25425: 304-535-6331

Mabry Mill Coffee & Craft Shop (Meadows of Dan):
   540-952-2947

Hilltop Restaurant (Meadows of Dan): 540-952-2326

10

Heading to The Homestead

Getting there: From Washington, take I-66 west about an hour to I-81. Take I-81 south about an hour to Staunton. The U.S. 250 exit begins the drive. From Richmond, take I-64 west about 100 miles to I-81 near Staunton. Take I-81 north to the first exit, U.S. 250, which is the beginning of the drive.

Highlights: Buckhorn Inn; George Washington National Forest; Highland Inn; Fort Lewis Lodge; Warm Springs; The Homestead; Goshen Pass. This drive can be completed in one day, but at least a long weekend is recommended.

You can always find a good reason for a country road drive. The lure of a winding road, a small town, a well-known restaurant, or a quaint bed-and-breakfast is reason enough to jump in the car. The Homestead is enough reason to take this drive.

The drive begins in the Shenandoah Valley town of Staunton (see Chapter 7), and U.S. 250 quickly changes into a winding country road. The mountains of the George Washington National Forest loom ahead.

Make sure to look for the Buckhorn Inn (a restored 1811 inn) near Churchville. The famous country buffet at this rustic establishment draws regulars from all over the state. Time your drive so that you can stop for lunch or supper, or stay the night in one of the inn's seven cozy rooms.

Past Churchville, the road leads into the heart of the George Washington National Forest and some serious elevation gains (and curvy roads). There aren't many pulloffs along this portion of the road, but you'll find some great views. The Highland County scenic overlook at 2,110 feet features Confederate breastworks dating back to 1862. Confederate troops built these fortifications to block Union soldiers who were advancing from the Shenandoah Valley. A short loop trail provides a view of the breastworks and the surrounding countryside.

After some major mountainous driving, the road finally heads out of the national forest and down into Monterey. This town is great for walking and exploring.

One highlight of Monterey is the Highland Inn, a classic 1904 Victorian inn on the National Historic Register. The inn offers 17 well-appointed rooms and gracious dining. We also liked the nearby Maple Restaurant.

The road to The Homestead begins with U.S. 220 south, which winds through farmland and past a rushing stream. About 20 miles out of Monterey, you enter Bath County and reenter the George Washington National Forest, which covers this entire area.

About 10 miles north of Warm Springs is the historic marker for Fort Lewis. The sign is seven miles east of what was known as Wilson's Fort, which was garrisoned in the fall of 1756 by Lt. Charles Lewis, younger brother of the famous Indian fighter Andrew Lewis.

The Fort Lewis Lodge off U.S. 220 is a great retreat during or after a long drive. John and Caryl Cowden offer a scenic setting, modernly rustic accommodations, great meals, and plenty to do. It's a perfect way to explore the forest if you have time.

The informative Bath County Visitors Center kiosk, located just outside Warm Springs, offers all sorts of tourist information. One highlight for us was the Warm Springs Pool, where you can soak in clean, clear 90°F water. The men's pool was built in 1761, and the original structure is still standing. The women's pool was built in 1836. Ask to see the "ducking chair," which enabled invalids to take the waters. Robert E. Lee's wife, Mary, a victim of rheumatoid arthritis, used this pool during visits to Warm Springs before the Civil War.

Across the street is the Warm Springs Inn. The brick shell was an early Bath County courthouse, with the old jail and a cell door carved by prisoners. The building became a country store, then the Maple Court Inn, and finally the Warm Springs Inn in the 1930s.

In town, our favorite place is The Inn at Gristmill Square. This "community" was created in 1972 using five original 19th-century buildings. A mill on Warm Springs Run has been located at this site since 1711.

The buildings now house wonderful guest rooms and suites, the Waterwheel Restaurant, the Simon Kenton Pub, the Country Stores, and the Bath and Tennis Club. The McWilliams family are great hosts, and the inn is a perfect place for a meal or much more.

The Homestead, our main destination, is a pretty five-mile drive from Warm Springs. As you drive downhill and into Hot Springs, The Homestead unfolds before you like a rich Oriental carpet.

This sprawling property is a southern-style resort steeped in tradition dating back to 1766, but with many modern touches. You enter another world when you pull up to the elegant entrance and allow the crisp staff to take care of your car and luggage. Leave your worries in your auto.

For more than 225 years, country road drivers have come to The Homestead to restore and refresh themselves in the

The Homestead resort

invigorating mountain air and soothing, healing waters. It was thought that the waters could cure or relieve the symptoms of ailments such as gout, rheumatism, arthritis, neuritis, lumbago, hypertension, nephritis, and nervous disorders.

Legend and local history say that The Homestead's hot springs were discovered by a Native American traveling through the mountains in the 16th century. He evidently found a spring of warm water, drank from it, slept, awoke the next day invigorated, and later spread the tale of his discovery.

Dr. Thomas Walker, an early explorer of the valley in 1750, wrote, "We went to Hot Springs . . . the spring is clear and warmer than new milk and there is a spring of cold water within twenty feet of the warm one." In 1755, George Washington visited Hot Springs while on an inspection tour of forts along the Allegheny frontier. Many travelers followed, and The Homestead was established and grew to accommodate them.

Check-in is just off the Great Hall, with its plush furnishings, many fireplaces, and lounging guests. Then you are led to your room, in great anticipation of the accommodations and views that await you there.

Homestead rooms are like those of a small country inn— cozy and thoughtfully decorated. There's so much to see and do, however, that you won't spend too much time there.

A weekend is not nearly long enough to enjoy all that The Homestead has to offer. Many pleasurable pursuits, both indoors and out, are available. It's just a matter of pursuing your passion.

Here's our short list of favorite Homestead activities: spa visits, shopping along Cottage Row, fishing in a mountain stream, skeet shooting, bowling, tennis in a beautiful setting, horseback riding, hiking, and skiing in winter. We discover a new passion to pursue every time we visit.

Golf is a big draw for many guests. Three courses are nestled in the Allegheny Mountains. The first tee at The

Homestead Course is the oldest in continuous use in the United States, having been built in 1892.

The Spa is often my favorite spot. Discovered more than four hundred years ago, the Hot Springs are legendary for their restorative powers. Built in 1892, The Spa was one of the first European-style spas and bathhouses in the United States. It's been completely renovated.

You can relax in the indoor or outdoor pools or go for the full treatment. The facility features a full-service hydrotherapeutic center offering various baths, a steam room, sauna, a salt glow, a Swiss shower, a scotch spray, massages, and much more. It's the ultimate way to relieve any driving stiffness.

Once you feel fit, it's time for a filling meal. The Dining Room features gourmet cuisine, with six-course classic menus, buffets, live entertainment, ballroom dancing, and a magnificent, sparkling chandelier. The Grille offers late-night dining in a casual atmosphere. Café Albert is a cozy coffeehouse that is great for pastries and lighter fare.

Our favorite place for casual meals at The Homestead is Sam Snead's Tavern, a converted bank where Virginia wines are stored in the antique walk-in vault. The casual atmosphere and menu make for a nice lunch or dinner. American favorites include New York Strip Steak, Virginia Allegheny Mountain Rainbow Trout, and The Tavern's Hickory Smoked Barbecued Spareribs (a messy and tasty treat).

The Homestead offers special weekend rates and packages. However, if your budget doesn't allow a stay there, you'll find many smaller bed-and-breakfasts and inns in the area.

Leaving The Homestead is a bit of a shock, but the surrounding countryside and beautiful driving make the transition a bit easier. Retrace your steps to Warm Springs, where you can pick up State 39, a Virginia Byway, which will take you to Lexington.

Much of the drive is along the Maury River, which can range from a babbling brook to a rushing river. This road offers many scenic pulloffs and chances to enjoy the sounds of the mountains and the water rolling along the rock-strewn river.

The town of Goshen is a nice stop halfway to Lexington. You can get a quick country meal at the Sunset Restaurant, the Cozy Corner restaurant, or the Mill Creek Café.

Another option is to put together a small picnic or snack and continue on to Goshen Pass. This pretty natural area features excellent pulloffs, public facilities, picnic tables, and great views of the towering mountains and the river cutting through them.

The drive goes through the small town of Rockbridge Baths, where Maury River Mercantile is a draw. The store offers groceries, gifts, a deli, and antiques. It also serves as a game-checking station and information bureau for local activities.

Lexington (see Chapter 7) is just ahead, past the Virginia Horse Center, the 1867 country manor Fassifern B&B, and finally too many fast-food joints and modern hotels. The Homestead is just a memory—until the next country road drive.

For More Information

Buckhorn Inn (Churchville): 540-337-6900

Highland Inn (Monterey): 540-468-2143

Fort Lewis Lodge (Millboro): 540-925-2314

Warm Springs Inn: 540-839-5351

The Inn at Gristmill Square (Warm Springs):
540-839-2231

The Homestead (Hot Springs): 540-839-5500, 800-336-5771
(out of state); 800-542-5734 (in Virginia); or 800-838-1776
(reservations)

The Fassifern B&B (Lexington): 540-463-1013

11

Southwest Virginia

Getting there: From Richmond, take I-64 west about 100 miles and then I-81 south about 200 miles to Marion. Then take State 16 (or State 16 and County 603) toward U.S. 58 to enjoy the Mount Rogers National Recreation Area. If you wish to skip the recreation area, take I-81 south directly to Abingdon and begin the U.S. 58 drive there.

Highlights: Scenery and hiking in the Mount Rogers National Recreation Area; Abingdon and the Martha Washington Inn; Natural Tunnel; Big Stone Gap; Cumberland Gap. You need at least two days to complete part or all of this drive.

Southwest Virginia often plays second fiddle to the rest of the Old Dominion, but only because of the long drive it typically takes to reach the area. Once there, explorers find a beautiful and peaceful region with interesting things to see and do.

The long drive down I-81 is worth the options you'll find off whichever exit you choose. Fans of mountain scenery should head for the Mount Rogers National Recreation Area. Small town lovers should start the drive in Abingdon.

Mount Rogers is the highest peak in Virginia, at 5,729 feet. The Mount Rogers Scenic Byway is the ideal way to explore this beautiful area. There are two options: County 603 from

Troutdale to Konnarock or U.S. 58 from Volney to Damascus. Either way eventually leads to Abingdon.

The Troutdale-to-Konnarock drive is about 13 miles and runs through the heart of the Mount Rogers National Recreation Area. Troutdale was once a bustling logging town but is now a quaint village that is the highest incorporated city east of the Mississippi River. Stay at the Fox Hill Inn, where innkeeper David Noe offers great rooms with a view. It's a perfect base for a full day of exploration. Ask David about the home of publisher and author Sherwood Anderson. The prolific writer, who had a big influence on Ernest Hemingway and William Faulkner, is buried in Round Hill Cemetery.

The drive west through Fairwood Valley features fascinating scenery and foliage. For campers and hikers, the large Grindstone Campground is just four miles down the road.

You'll find many photo opportunities along this stretch. Look for the Bethel Baptist Church and the Log Church in the three-mile section after the campground.

Great views of Mount Rogers are often available along this part of the drive. It stands out because of its prominent spruce and fir cap. Many access trails lead to the peak.

Konnarock was once the site of a large lumber mill and an active community. Look for the Lutheran Girls School, a former boarding school sided with chestnut bark, and the Lutheran Church, made entirely of stone. County 603 intersects U.S. 58 just past Konnarock.

The Volney-to-Damascus stretch of U.S. 58 is a busier road, with rolling countryside and excellent access to the Mount Rogers National Recreation Area. About 10 miles east of Volney, you'll find Grayson Highlands State Park, which offers year-round access to the area. It's a great place for hiking and other state-sponsored outdoor activities.

About four miles past the entrance to the park, look for the Mount Rogers School. This is one of the few remaining schools in the nation that teaches kindergarten through 12th grade in one building. It has the smallest high-school enrollment in the state.

Hikers should take County 600 north to Whitetop Mountain and Elk Garden Gap. The road leads to a parking area and the shortest hike to the top of Mount Rogers. This trail is only four-and-a-half miles long and well worth the trip.

The drive along the southwest slope of Whitetop Mountain (it's often covered with snow or frost) features acres of Christmas trees. This region is famous for the production of beautiful trees, and the drive will put you in the holiday spirit at any time of the year. The Beartree Recreation Area is one of the most modern places in the state to camp, fish, or swim.

This stretch of U.S. 58 also offers glimpses of the famous Virginia Creeper Trail. This 34-mile hiking trail was once a major Indian trace leading from present-day North Carolina to the Ohio River. An old railroad bed now offers a perfect path for hiking, biking, horseback riding, or cross-country skiing. Look for some of the 32 rustic railroad trestles crossing the many gorges and rivers in the area.

Damascus marks the end of an exploration of the Mount Rogers area. This active town is a popular supply stop for Appalachian Trail hikers and is fast becoming a center for all sorts of outdoor sports. From Damascus, it's a quick drive to Abingdon and a real introduction to southwest Virginia.

Make plans to stay in Abingdon for at least one night, and try to stay at the Martha Washington Inn. The Martha, as it's affectionately called, was originally built in 1832 by Gen. Francis Preston. There is even an old soldier's song about the inn:

> If you want to find a true school,
> Come to Martha;
> Housed within a mansion old
> Where traditions oft are told
> Of the soldier lovers bold;
> Up at Martha.

An $8 million renovation has made this an elegantly hospitable retreat and a perfect base for southwest Virginia explorations. Situated right on Main Street, the hotel features antiques, four-poster canopied beds, and many reminders of the past, as well as the modern amenities of a luxury hotel. The rooms, service, and dining are well worth the trip to this far corner of Virginia, and the hotel serves as a haven at the end of the long drive.

Ask some of the older staff members about the Martha's history, including the hotel's time as a girls' school; the legend of the riderless Yankee horse; the Civil War soldier loved and protected by a local schoolgirl but ultimately slain; and illustrious visitors such as Eleanor Roosevelt, Harry Truman, Lady Bird Johnson, Jimmy Carter, and Elizabeth Taylor.

The town of Abingdon is packed with history and quaint shops. A walk along Main Street is a pleasant way to spend a few hours.

The first stop should be the Barter Theatre. This historic playhouse evolved when Robert Porterfield gathered a troupe of unemployed actors in 1933. They exchanged theater tickets for produce, livestock, and other goods brought in by local people. Today the Barter Theatre is the State Theatre of Virginia. Try to catch a performance (from spring to fall).

Abingdon's walking tour brochure is a great way to explore the town's historic buildings, many of which have excellent explanatory markers. I found the William King House, the Washington County Courthouse, and the Dunn's Hotel/Virginia House particularly interesting.

Abingdon serves as the beginning of an exploration of southwest Virginia along U.S. 58. Take U.S. 11 or I-81 south toward Bristol and get on U.S. 58 west.

The rolling countryside and scenic beauty begin almost immediately. In 1775, Daniel Boone made a road through Big Moccasin Gap all the way to Boonesboro, Kentucky. The road follows an original Indian path and was known as the Wilderness Trail from the east to Kentucky. The area has produced proud mountain folk, and this country road offers a glimpse into their lives.

After passing between Weber City and Gate City, U.S. 58 heads for Natural Tunnel State Park. Just outside Duffield, Natural Tunnel is a huge underground tunnel formed more than one million years ago from the dissolving of limestone and dolomitic bedrock by groundwater bearing carbonic acid. Later, the flow of Stock Creek enlarged the opening, which is now more than 400 feet high.

Natural Tunnel can be reached by a seasonal (and steep) chairlift or by a stroll down the tunnel trail. The overlook is awe-inspiring, but the view from the observation platform at the mouth of the tunnel is definitely worth the trip. The new visitors center is a great place to go for further information about the "Eighth Wonder of the World."

It's hard to stay on U.S. 58 with so much to see, and Big Stone Gap is one of the diversions. Just 15 miles north on U.S. 23, Big Stone Gap offers an entire day of interesting possibilities. Check out the Car 101 Tourist Information Center as you head into town. It's located in a restored 1891 Pullman car.

Big Stone Gap is famous for its outdoor drama *Trail of the Lonesome Pine*. This play tells the love story of a Virginia mountain girl and a handsome mining engineer from the East. It depicts the great coal and iron ore days of the region in a dramatic way. The play runs from mid-June through Labor Day on Thursdays, Fridays, and Saturdays.

Next door to the small outdoor theater on Clinton Avenue is the Jane Tolliver House and Craft Shop. The heroine of the drama lived in this pretty house while attending school nearby. The home now features restored 19th-century furnishings and a collection of local crafts. I loved letting the women in the shop regale me with stories about the crafts and the people who make them.

In the center of Big Stone Gap, the John Fox, Jr. Museum serves as a memorial to the author of *Trail of the Lonesome Pine*. His novel was the first to sell a million copies in the United States. The house was built in 1888 and contains Fox family furnishings and memorabilia.

Modern-day explorers shouldn't miss the Southwest Virginia Museum on Wood Avenue, housed in a beautiful home built of local limestone and sandstone. This intriguing state-run museum depicts the pioneer life and development of Big Stone Gap and the region. The informative displays and artifacts provide insight into the history of the area, and visitors depart with a new appreciation of southwest Virginia. I think it's one of the state's finest museums.

Other interesting stops in Big Stone Gap include the Harry W. Meador, Jr. Coal Museum, the Victorian homes of Poplar Hill, and the memorial at Miner's Park (the town is known as the "Gateway to the Coalfields"). With all this history, Big Stone Gap is definitely worth the diversion from U.S. 58. If you have time for a meal, head for the Mutual Pharmacy on Wood Avenue. This typical smalltown store and eatery is a wonderful way to meet the locals.

Back in Duffield, U.S. 58 continues on 54 miles to Cumberland Gap. Small towns like Dot, Rose Hill, and Ewing sit in the shadows of Powell Mountain and, later, Cumberland Mountain. But Cumberland Gap is the draw, just as it has been for centuries.

Before people passed through Cumberland Gap, migratory animals used the break in the Appalachian Mountains to move west in search of food. Native Americans followed the animals into the rich hunting grounds of Kentucky, and this trail of trade and warfare became known as the Warrior's Path.

Daniel Boone came to the area in 1775 and, with 30 men, marked out the Wilderness Trail from Cumberland Gap into Kentucky. Mass immigration through the gap began, with 12,000 people crossing into the new territory by the end of the Revolutionary War and another 100,000 by the time Kentucky was admitted to the Union in 1792.

Today Cumberland Gap is a major tourist attraction and well worth the drive. The gap is situated at the convergence of Virginia, Kentucky, and Tennessee. To get information about the area, it's best to head out of Virginia for a brief stop at the Cumberland Gap Visitor Center and Park Headquarters in Middlesboro, Kentucky.

Highlights of a drive to and around the Cumberland Gap National Historical Park include more than 50 miles of hiking trails, excellent camping and picnicking facilities, the Hensley Settlement on Brush Mountain, and simply incredible views. The switchback Pinnacle Road up to Pinnacle Overlook is well worth the drive, with a 2,440-foot view over three states (there's a great picture-taking spot where you can straddle the Virginia-Kentucky state line).

Cumberland Gap marks the end of the Virginia portion of the Wilderness Road, but it was only the beginning for settlers heading west. You can head east on U.S. 58 back to Abingdon, or you can make a country road loop by taking Alternate U.S. 58 from Jonesville through Pennington Gap, Big Stone Gap, and Norton, then back to Abingdon.

This pretty drive through the Jefferson National Forest

features another chance to visit Big Stone Gap. Head for Flag Rock or High Knob to enjoy some of Virginia's best views.

For More Information

Mount Rogers National Recreation Area (Marion): 540-783-5196

Fox Hill Inn (Troutdale): 800-874-3313

Grayson Highlands State Park (Mouth of Wilson): 540-579-7092

Abingdon Convention & Visitors Bureau: 540-676-2282

Martha Washington Inn (Abingdon): 540-628-3161 or 800-533-1014

Barter Theatre (Abingdon): 540-628-3991

Natural Tunnel State Park (Scott County): 540-940-2674

Car 101 Tourist Information Center (Big Stone Gap): 540-523-2060

Trail of the Lonesome Pine Outdoor Drama (Big Stone Gap): 540-523-1235

Southwest Virginia Museum (Big Stone Gap): 540-523-1322

Cumberland Gap National Historical Park (Middlesboro, KY): 606-248-2817

12

Backcountry by the Beach

Getting there: From Virginia Beach, take Pacific Avenue out of the resort area across Rudee Inlet. This turns into General Booth Boulevard and the start of the drive.

Highlights: Virginia Beach Marine Science Museum; vegetable and fruit stands; Sandbridge; Pungo; backcountry beach scenery.

Most people don't associate a country road drive with a beach resort, but Virginia Beach veterans like us have learned that there is much more to this legendary hot spot than hitting the beach. This drive is just one of the many pleasures we've found when we aren't enjoying resort life.

You leave Virginia Beach by way of Pacific Avenue south. The commercialization of the beach is sometimes overwhelming, but you'll find some small gems just off this well-traveled road. Right before the Rudee Inlet bridge is a super restaurant called Rudee's on the Inlet. It's great for people watching as well as fresh seafood.

The stretch of General Booth Boulevard beyond the bridge has been built up, but one major highlight just after Rudee Inlet is the Virginia Marine Science Museum. This is one of the state's most interesting museums and is a great place to explore for those who are young at heart. Through exhibits and special tours and shows, the lively museum gives visitors an inside look at Virginia's marine environment.

After several more miles of shopping centers and fast-food joints, the neon lights and billboards give way to farmland. Princess Anne Road toward Sandbridge and Pungo is a left turn into a different kind of day at the beach.

Virginia Beach's city limits actually extend south all the way to the North Carolina border, encompassing thousands of acres of farmland, wildlife refuges, barrier islands, open beaches, and much more. Princess Anne Road follows the Pungo Ridge, which is an ancient dune line where sand is still mined for beach replenishment and other projects.

The winding road leads to a lively intersection where Davis Farm Produce draws locals and visitors from afar with its fresh fruits and vegetables. We always check out the current crop as a scouting mission for purchases on our way back.

From the intersection, many people head to Sandbridge. This beach "town" sits right on the Atlantic Ocean and is dotted with several hundred weatherworn rental cottages. The beach life here is a direct contrast to that in Virginia Beach proper in that it's more relaxed and much less commercial.

The Back Bay National Wildlife Refuge, south of Sandbridge, is a great place to explore on foot. It contains about 4,600 acres of beaches, dunes, woodlands, and marshes, with many opportunities to observe wildlife, hike, and participate in back-to-nature activities.

Back on Princess Anne Road, the drive continues on to downtown Pungo. Pungo was established as a town in 1870 and was annexed by the city in 1963. The area was originally occupied by Native Americans, and many artifacts dating back more than 3,000 years have been found.

Pungo Produce features fresh, locally grown produce. We usually compare prices with Davis Farm Produce, but we always buy a snack of fruits or vegetables.

Across the street is Munden's Downtown Pungo Bar. This hopping joint makes for a fun nighttime outing from Virginia

Beach or Sandbridge. A small grocery store is attached to it, and the friendly staff will provide local lore and sightseeing recommendations.

Just around the corner is my favorite place in Pungo (and in the Virginia Beach area)—the Pungo Fish House, which sells fresh fish and tasty crabs. If you've never eaten crabs before, this is the place to start. You can buy them live and prepare them yourself, but we prefer to let the cooks at the fish house spice and steam the blue crabs for us. We buy a few dozen or a bushel and head back to our hotel or cottage to eat them while they're still hot.

If you have an urgent hunger, head to the Pungo Grill, just down the main drag. The historic 1919 building is a great setting for a meal, and the restaurant also offers peaceful outdoor patio dining. The eclectic menu includes seafood, pasta, and fresh vegetables. I particularly like some of the Cajun specialties prepared with local seafood.

Nearby is Fran's Antiques. Fran has a little of everything, from serious antiques to just plain interesting stuff. Her store is large, friendly, and fun to explore. I rarely get out of there without buying something.

The road south of Pungo continues through more farmland. Watch for the left-hand turn to Davis Farm. During several harvest seasons, the farm offers pick-your-own specials. The strawberry season is especially popular with pickers, who create a colorful scene as they pick the luscious red fruits.

You'll also come upon a few nurseries. Stop in if you're looking for just the right plant grown under ideal conditions.

For More Information

Rudee's on the Inlet (Virginia Beach): 757-425-1777

Virginia Marine Science Museum (Virginia Beach):
    757-437-4949

Back Bay National Wildlife Refuge (Virginia Beach): 757-721-2412

Munden's Downtown Pungo Bar: 757-426-2701

Pungo Fish House: 757-426-6808

Pungo Grill: 757-426-6655

Fran's Antiques (Pungo): 757-426-3360 or 757-721-6109 (home)

13

The Eastern Shore

Getting there: From Washington, D.C., take U.S. 50 east through Annapolis to the Maryland portion of the Eastern Shore. Continue through Maryland on U.S. 50 to U.S. 13. Once in Virginia, take State 175 east to Chincoteague, where you can start the Eastern Shore drive from the north (the description in this chapter starts from the south). From Richmond, take I-64 east to U.S. 13 near Norfolk. This leads to the Chesapeake Bay Bridge-Tunnel and the start of the drive at the tip of the Eastern Shore.

Highlights: Chesapeake Bay Bridge-Tunnel; Cape Charles; Eastville; Pungoteague; Wachapreague; Onancock; Chincoteague; Assateague Island; Eastern Shore Escapes. This drive can be completed in one long day, but it's better to spend a weekend or more exploring the Eastern Shore.

The Eastern Shore is a totally different kind of Virginia and a country road lover's trip of a lifetime. The people, places, and food make this land between the Chesapeake Bay and the Atlantic Ocean a unique experience. In his book *Chesapeake* James Michener described the area this way: "It was simply there, the indefinable river, now broad, now narrow, in this age turbulent, in that asleep, becoming a formidable stream and then a spacious bay and then the ocean itself, an unbroken chain with all parts so interrelated that it will exist forever."

Virginia's Eastern Shore is steeped in history. From the Native Americans (many towns have Indian names) to centuries-old fishing villages (many towns have names from the sea), the Eastern Shore has evolved into one of the state's most interesting destinations.

Coming from Richmond, our drive started with the Chesapeake Bay Bridge-Tunnel and headed north. Many drivers from the Washington, D.C., area will start from the north and head south. Either way, you'll use busy U.S. 13 as the base for excursions off the busy road.

The Chesapeake Bay Bridge-Tunnel was opened in 1964 and is one of the engineering wonders of the world. It runs 17.5 miles across the Chesapeake Bay, with two tunnels of one mile each and the rest a two-lane bridge (a second parallel bridge opened in 1998).

Drivers can stop at the South Island turnoff, 3.3 miles from the Virginia Beach shore, for a great view in both directions. This is the only official stopping place along the bridge-tunnel. The stop also features a gift shop, restaurant, and busy fishing pier (the concrete piles attract a lot of fish).

On a clear day, you can see the Eastern Shore for miles before the end of the bridge-tunnel. The North Channel Bridge rises 80 feet above the water, so local fishermen can pursue their catch on either side.

After the bridge, look for Fisherman's Island, a quiet wildlife refuge where no stops or visitors are allowed. Off to the right, the Cape Charles Lighthouse has been putting out the strongest light on the Eastern Shore since 1895. The Eastern Shore of Virginia National Wildlife Refuge is also off to the right on County 600.

Cape Charles provides a great introduction to the Eastern Shore. This town was once the biggest city on the peninsula.

The railroad and harbor contributed to an economic boom that lasted until the 1950s. When the railroad left, so did much of the shipping activity, so the town went into decline.

Cape Charles is now experiencing a rebirth, as many people are renovating the beautiful buildings left over from the boom. A drive around town reveals many beautiful houses and stores. Farther afield, little fishing villages like Oyster and Cherrystone provide a glimpse of Eastern Shore life.

A few of our favorite places in Cape Charles include Charmar's Country Store (213 Mason Avenue), the scenic Boardwalk, Sunset View (2 Randolph Avenue), the "Houses That Grew Together," and several Sears, Roebuck houses (1 and 3 Randolph Avenue, 8 Monroe Avenue, and 225 Jefferson Avenue).

If you would like to explore more of Cape Charles or want a peaceful place to stay before or after the drive, check out the Sea Gate B&B. Hosts Chris and Jim welcome guests to this beautifully restored home.

Back on U.S. 13, you'll see more commercial activity, which continues all the way north to the Maryland border. Although the side roads are much more interesting, U.S. 13 does feature some great places to buy local seafood and fresh produce.

Eastville is the next town of interest, at a well-marked left turn off the highway (U.S. 13 Business Route, on which you can continue north to return to U.S. 13 proper). Historic Eastville features many beautiful homes, government buildings, and churches. All are within an easy stroll or drive of the pretty Courthouse Green. If it's time for a meal, try the old Eastville Inn.

At County 607, take a right and follow the signs for Accomack Vineyards. We love Virginia wines, and this is the Eastern Shore's only winery. The sandy soil and local climate

have made for some interesting white
wines, as well as fun tours and tast-
ings.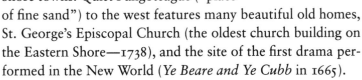
    State 180 leads off U.S. 13 in both
directions to typical old Eastern
Shore towns. Quiet Pungoteague ("place
of fine sand") to the west features many beautiful old homes,
St. George's Episcopal Church (the oldest church building on
the Eastern Shore—1738), and the site of the first drama performed in the New World (*Ye Beare and Ye Cubb* in 1665).
    Busier Wachapreague ("little city by the sea") to the east
is popular with fishermen. The waterfront and quaint streets
are great for walking. We also enjoyed a quick bite to eat at
the Island House restaurant at the docks. Wachapreague features a wonderful little bed-and-breakfast called the Burton
House.
    Back on U.S. 13, take a left onto State 179 and head into
Onancock ("foggy place"), one of our favorite Eastern Shore
finds. The town is the second largest community on Virginia's
Eastern Shore. It is steeped in history and waterfront life.
Pretty Market Street leads to the quiet Wharf, where you'll
find the Hopkins & Brothers Store, opened in 1842 and now
a Virginia Historic Landmark. Along with the store there's
also a nice restaurant upstairs.
    The Wharf is also the embarkation point for Tangier
Island Cruises. If you have time, take a boat over to Tangier
Island, first sighted by Captain John Smith in 1608. This small
island has remained relatively unchanged for decades. The
proud residents welcome visitors to the quiet, narrow streets
and a simpler way of life.
    Back in Onancock, head for Kerr Place (pronounced
"Carr"), a beautiful old brick home that serves as the offices
and museum of the Eastern Shore of Virginia Historical
Society. Onancock has many pretty churches and homes,

including the Colonial Manor Inn, one of the few true tourist homes left on the Eastern Shore.

Continue north on U.S. 13 to State 176 to Parksley. This planned Victorian-style community offers tree-lined streets, pretty homes, and the Eastern Shore of Virginia Railway Museum for railroad buffs.

The rest of U.S. 13 is a commercial prelude to one of the best areas on the Eastern Shore: Chincoteague and Assateague Island. Turn right onto State 175 for a country road drive to another world.

On the left of State 175, it's hard to miss huge Wallops Island. The main base on the mainland and the Wallops Island launch facility are run by NASA. The area has played a vital role in the nation's space program since the first rocket launch there on July 4, 1945.

The only part of the Wallops Island facility usually open to the public is the Visitor Center. This new center is interesting for all those who are young at heart, with space-oriented displays, model rockets, and much more.

Modern Wallops Island is a direct contrast to Chincoteague, an Eastern Shore town from another era. Chincoteague means "beautiful land across the water," and this is still true today.

Chincoteague is an island community based on the water and tourism. Quaint Main Street and many side streets are great for dining and shopping. Several annual events also are held here. Only a stay of several days will provide ample time to explore the town.

Some of our favorite discoveries include the Island Roxy Theatre (203 South Main Street), the Chincoteague Volunteer Fire Company (South Main Street at Cropper Street), the Carnival Grounds (570 South Main Street), Island Arts (6196

Maddox Boulevard), and the Main Street Shop & Gallery (4282 North Main Street).

We stayed at a wonderful new bed-and-breakfast called the Watson House. This stunningly restored country Victorian home was built by Robert Watson in the late 1800s. It's right on Main Street, close to the carnival grounds, restaurants, and shopping.

Tom and Jacque Derrickson and David and JoAnne Snead are the innkeepers at the Watson House. They offer six nice rooms, all with private baths, as well as a delicious breakfast and friendly advice for exploring. We stayed in the beautiful Bayview Room, but all of the rooms are perfect.

If the Watson House is full, Chincoteague offers all sorts of other accommodations—bed-and-breakfasts, cottages, hotels, and even camping.

Seafood is at the top of almost every menu in Chincoteague. Start an evening meal at the Landmark Crab House along North Main Street. This restaurant features stunning sunsets on the deck and super seafood.

Other great restaurants in Chincoteague include Spinnaker's, Beachway, A.J.'s, Steamer's, and the elegantly casual Channel Bass Inn. The Watson House has most of the menus, comments from past guests, and the innkeepers' own personal favorites.

If you've never picked crabs, just ask your server for a quick lesson in this wonderfully tasty (and messy) experience. Diners who fall in love with the famed blue crabs and other fruits of the Chesapeake Bay should stop at one of the roadside stands or stores for a tasty souvenir of the trip (just make sure to buy enough ice).

One of the biggest draws to Chincoteague is the Chincoteague Volunteer Firemen's Carnival. This annual event is held the first two weekends in July, as well as throughout the last two weeks of the month. In a throwback to bygone days, the carnival grounds feature nightly rides, attractions, games, food, music, and more.

The annual Pony Swim and Pony Auction late in the month draw thousands of visitors from around the world. The wild ponies of Assateague Island were made famous in Marguerite Henry's *Misty of Chincoteague*. Her beautiful narrative describes the area well: "The people moved their homes and their churches to nearby Chincoteague Island, for Assateague belonged to the wild things—to the wild birds that nested on it, and the wild ponies whose ancestors had lived on it since the days of the Spanish galleon."

Each year, many of these ponies are herded into a corral on the south end of Assateague. On Wednesday of the last week in July, the ponies are herded across the channel to Chincoteague by local firefighters. The next day, they are driven down Main Street for the annual auction.

All the proceeds from the carnival and auction go to the Chincoteague Volunteer Fire Company general fund for maintenance and replacement of equipment and for emergency use for the benefit of the entire community.

Just across another bridge, the Chincoteague National Wildlife Refuge sits on the southern end of Assateague Island. This pristine seashore environment is still much as it has been for centuries. Assateague Island also encompasses Maryland's equally beautiful Assateague State Park.

The Chincoteague National Wildlife Refuge has much to explore. It was established in 1943 as a wintering area for migratory wildfowl, but it has become much more. It's a haven for beach lovers, hikers, bikers, bird-watchers, and wild pony-watchers. Many excellent nature programs are offered.

Stop at the Chincoteague Refuge Center for information and schedules. Our favorite spots on the island include the huge lighthouse, the bike paths, the beach, and anywhere you can see deer or wild ponies.

For More Information

Virginia's Eastern Shore Tourism Commission (Melfa):
757-787-2460

Chesapeake Bay Bridge-Tunnel (Cape Charles): 757-331-2960

Sea Gate B&B (Cape Charles): 757-331-2206

Island House (Wachapreague): 757-787-4242

Burton House (Wachapreague): 757-787-4560

Tangier Island Cruises (Onancock): 757-891-2240

Colonial Manor Inn (Onancock): 757-787-3521

Eastern Shore of Virginia Railway Museum (Parksley):
757-665-RAIL

Wallops Island Visitor Center (Wallops Island): 757-824-2298

Chincoteague Chamber of Commerce: 757-336-6161

Watson House (Chincoteague): 757-336-1564

Landmark Crab House (Chincoteague): 757-336-5552

Chincoteague National Wildlife Refuge: 757-336-6122

Index